YSTORY®

The Real Truth About Gen Y

And What It Means For Marketers

YSTORY®

The Real Truth About Gen Y

And What It Means For Marketers

RTM&J Real Truth Marketing & Joy®

Stephen Hom

Printed by Global Book Publishing, Charleston, SC, USA

October 2009

ISBN: 1-4392-5911-9

Bulk order requests can be requested by emailing info@rtmj.com. If you would like to reach RTM&J regarding potential consulting and/or speaking assignments, please email info@rtmj.com or call 770-225-6801. You can learn more about RTM&J at www.rtmj.com.

FOR MARKETERS WHO NEED TO KNOW.

CONTENTS

RTM&J Real Truth Marketing & Joy LLC

PREFACE

Admit it. I don't really know and understand Gen Y.

I don't know what they think, how they feel, and what they do. I just don't get it. This is what I said to myself during a conversation with Jayne, my then 17-year old daughter; or, maybe she said this to me. In any event, I am a professional marketer and strategist: I am supposed to be able to get her head, empathize with her heart, and influence her behavior. And yet, at the time, I couldn't.

Generation gaps have always existed. But what about her generation was I not understanding? What didn't I know? As I thought about this question, a larger question emerged: **What do marketers need to know about this powerful upcoming generation?** And, with that question, the process which led to this book began.

For me, generational targeting has always been somewhat of a disconnect. Just because someone belongs to a cohort of age-peers, doesn't mean they necessarily can be treated as one market. Generally, I consider need-states as a basis for segmentation and then overlay emotive connections, geodemographics, lifestyle/stage, and so forth. Certainly, targeting a *generation* seems odd at best.

And, we're not suggesting that here. What we are saying is that typically a generation *is a generation* because its formative years are spent responding and reacting to a similar set of situations and circumstances. And it is this that provides the common thread and backdrop to their lives. So learning about Gen Y is more about understanding a culture derived from current events than it is about undergoing a formal segmentation process.

However, certainly the sets of situations and circumstances that arise during one's formative childhood years are not the only driver of personality and cohort traits. Can you guess who said the following?

"The children now love luxury; they have bad manners, contempt for authority; they show disrespect for elders... They

contradict their parents... and tyrannize their teachers."

No, it wasn't said of Gen Y, or Gen X, the Boomers or even The Greatest Generation. It is attributed to Socrates by Plato! Indeed, to some extent generations are just what they've always been. So why is it necessary to study Gen Y? **It's simple: because overall, Gen Y shops, communicates and consumes differently than past generations.** The advancement of the internet and social media has led them to become the most advanced openly communicative generations ever. And, unless we as marketers know and understand them we will not connect and our products, services, and messages will be irrelevant.

Although much has been written about Gen Y, this is one of the first books about this important consumer segment written by a Gen Yer, RTM&J's Stephen Hom.

RTM&J's Ystory® practice area is based on what makes Generation Y different: stories.

Watching Jayne grow up, I was amazed that she would lock and hide her diary in her room **but put her entire life's story on the internet for all to see.** She would instant message about things with friends that she'd never say in person. She opened her heart through posting poems and blurbs first on Xanga®, then MySpace®, then Facebook®.

Jayne has had more cell phones than shoes and yet uses them to text rather than talk. It is her wrist watch, her jewelry, her *life*. Being grounded? No big deal. Take away her cell phone, her link to the outside world – forget about it.

Facebook® and other social media sites have revolutionized this generation's self-image. When I think back over my high school and college years, I have a few iconic scenes and photos that help me remember the details. **This generation is creating their own personal documentary posted in real time.** How will they synthesize their own very existence when they have thousands of tagged photos, hundreds of "friends," and countless stories written for the world to see?

But enough about my interpretations of Gen Y. **What is important is that we understand Gen Yers from their point of view.** And so I challenged Stephen Hom, a then 20 years old RTM&J intern, to create and illustrate the basic elements of Ystory®.

Stephen dove into the Ystory® project and never looked back. He completed the due diligence required of any consultant and then put his spin on what it all meant.

Although it's largely one point of view, Stephen reached out to other Gen Yers for input by creating a Ystory® Facebook® page and sending out Zoomerang® surveys. You'll find their input in quotation marks throughout the book.

I was very careful not to impose my thinking or perspectives on the content of this book. To be honest, it had to be the real perspective in the voice of a Gen Yer. Certainly this book does not describe every Gen Yer or every sub-segment within the total group. And, that's ok.

I would like to **thank the following Gen Yers for their involvement** with the book: Stephen Hom, Cris Dizon, Elyse Preiss, Daniel Wise, Ruth Yang, Cameron Oddone, Meredith Lichtenstein, Rachel Fudman, Rebecca Perch, Austin Reynolds, Catherine Midkiff, Erik Hoffman, Esther Kim, Michael Dean, Arthur Moore, Felicia Edlin, Hudson Christian, Ryan King, Eun Sol Lee, Matt Nguyen, Stephanie Park, and Peter Yang. And, of course, my beautiful and smart Gen Y daughter Jayne for her inspiration.

Wishing you joy,
Rhonda Harper
Managing Partner & CEO

GET TO WHAT'S REAL

WHY WE MATTER

Generation Y is growing up, they're telling stories, and they're consuming at unprecedented levels. The most open and communications savvy generation yet, the Gen Y market represents a crucial opportunity for companies that want to become and stay relevant and competitive in the marketplace. In order to be prepared to target the largest generation ever, you need to know their story before you can tell them yours.

The Ystory® concept defines and describes Generation Y in detail and provides a profile with which to better target and reach this group of consumers. Gen Y is all about stories, and this profile gives each component of the story to highlight different key aspects about this group. This generation is formidable in size, spending power, and influence. Companies must better understand the way this group thinks, feels, and subsequently acts in order to capitalize on the opportunity Gen Y comprises.

Does Size Really Matter? People all over the globe have debated this age-old question since the beginning of time. In this case, **size indeed matters**. Gen Y is, quite simply, a huge generation, and they're making their formidable presence known.

Gen Y is loosely regarded as the cohort born between the early 1980s and the mid 1990s. However, many have Gen Y ranging from as early as 1978 to as late as 2000. The U.S. Census estimates Gen Y at around 83 million. They're the kids of the Baby Boomers, matching them in size and far outnumbering Gen X. With 83 million consumers coming of age and hitting the market hard, size certainly matters. Of that 83 million, fifty million range from the ages 18 to 29. This is a big number with even bigger implications. More than half of Gen Y is in the "adult" category and making their own purchase decisions. This adult segment knows what they want, does their price and product research before hand, and won't take anything less than a good deal. Even the younger segment of Gen Y knows what they want and are not afraid to vocalize this to their parents. And make no mistake – they want it all. Kids in Gen Y don't want a simple flip phone anymore; they want a fully loaded Blackberry or iPhone.

With the core of this generation at a current age of anywhere from eighteen to twenty-five, Gen Y is supporting themselves and living on their own, embracing adulthood, earning degrees, gaining work experience, and increasing their spending power.

General consensus puts Gen Y's spending power anywhere from two to three-hundred billion dollars in 2008, a gigantic figure that only continues to grow.

Moreover, experts estimate Gen Y's real influence as three to five times its direct spending power. Families and older friends are consulting this new generation more than ever on a vast array of purchasing decisions because Gen Y is so knowledgeable regarding new products and technology. Gen Y grew up engulfed in consumerism, and they've come out experts on the matter. Whether telling mom to buy a new digital camera or helping dad get a new laptop, Gen Yers' true effect is greater and spreads farther than just their own spending power.

Gen Y openly embraces this influence, too. They relish the ability to influence others and thoroughly enjoy their increasing financial independence. Gen Y spends big on anything and everything that makes their lives cooler, easier, and better, and with control over how much they spend and where they spend it, Gen Y is coming into its own as serious consumers and influencers in the market.

When it comes to this generation, size certainly does matter. Gen Y is big, with big money, and that has some big implications. Gen Y is unique, and loves its uniqueness. Unlike Gen X's cynical and pragmatic nature, Gen Y is optimistic, confident, ambitious, and yet naïve. Unlike their Baby

Boomer parents, who were experimental, individualistic, and free spirited, Gen Y are team-oriented, family-centric, and mainstream to the core. Gen X kids were "latchkey kids," but Gen Y kids had "helicopter parents," hovering over them incessantly. The vast array of generational influences have shaped this generation differently than any other, leading to a number of truly distinctive and descriptive characteristics that comprise the very core of this group.

GEN Y CHARACTERISTICS

While Gen Y is a fragmented and sometimes contradictory generation, a few main descriptive characteristics encompass a large part of Gen Y's core identity. So before diving into Gen Y's story, it is necessary to understand these characteristics, as they play an important underlying role in Gen Y's attitudes, behaviors, and lifestyles.

For better or for worse, Gen Y focuses strongly on its image and social stature. They are extremely self-aware, always knowing how they look, how people might see them, what trends are rising and how they fit in or stand out. This generation wants others to notice and remember them, and they want to feel connected to others; Gen Y heavily turns to image and status to achieve this delicate balance. This image consciousness and desire to please and be accepted leads to Gen Yers often acting as surface supporters instead of revolutionaries, head-nodders instead of neck-wringers. Being looked up to and both setting and following trends from an image and social standpoint are significant determinants in Gen Y members being important and cool, and because of this, Gen Y takes image extremely seriously. It's all about looking, feeling, and being creative and unique; conformity is taboo. **These Gen Yers value**

individuality while still wanting community, consensus, and a chance to communicate with others who understand them and who will listen and relate to them.

Gen Yers; tendencies to be storytellers reiterate that desire for others to notice, remember, and like them. With fragmented, fast-paced lives and the constant juggle of multiple goals and desires, with new, convenient channels to reach more people faster than ever before, Gen Y is not shy about expressing its voice to entertain and impress others. **Having a widespread influence means being seen as important, and the recording of one's stories is reassuring evidence that Gen Y members are being heard.** This generation is not revolutionary, breaking down doors with fiery opinions. Gen Y isn't the loudest group; they're not protesters, not boat rockers. Instead, they're a group with common, accepted beliefs who search for and thrive in communities of people who share those beliefs. Storytelling then – sharing tastes, beliefs, causes, and backgrounds – becomes a way to express oneself and find support and acceptance from others.

The seamless connection between technology and personal life for Gen Y enables them to tell all of these personal stories online and through new technologies in ways that reach more people instantly. Unlike other generations, Gen Y has grown up from the start with the internet, laptops, and camera phones, and thus technology has become an extremely personal tool that facilitates self-expression and comprises one's lifestyle. The computer is no longer a work tool, but rather personal entertainment and a vehicle to express one's passions and identity. Technology is not just a tool but also a connection to the rest of the world, a connection that is personal and vital to Gen Y's relevance and ability to leave its mark. It influences everything Gen Y does and has shaped their norms, communication habits, and lifestyle trends.

With this personal connection to technology and instant sharing comes the expectation and demand for immediate rewards and satisfaction. Gen Y shows its impatient streak in wanting to see the outcome and reward of everything before volunteering to put forth too much effort, work, and time. From digital cameras to email capability on phones, instant communication and gratification are the norm for this group. They received lots of attention as kids and familiar with getting what they want. Web page taking a few extra seconds to load? Gen Y will go to a different one. Gen Y is all about enjoying the benefits right away. They love experiences that give a higher value and relevant takeaway that can allow them to feel immediately more enriched and enlightened. **Gen Y prefers experience to anything.** That is "pay first, consume later" because the benefit of an experience occurs simultaneously with the effort put forth. Only when Gen Y can immediately enjoy the benefit will they put forth the effort. Patience? There's none here.

Lastly, if Gen Y feels like a promise to provide these enriching, rewarding experiences is empty, they'll be gone in an instant. As a group so accustomed to marketing and advertising bombarding them, Gen Y wants raw and real, not airbrushed and staged. Still relatively new to adulthood, Gen Y is proving itself and wants others to take them seriously and treat them with respect. They're a confident group, and they want to be engaged in an intelligent and genuine way before they'll be willing to give back. They're experts at sniffing out the tiniest lack of sincerity, and they'll make that insincerity known. Whether from friends, family, or corporations, Gen Y wants and expects respect and a genuine approach.

Gen Y is often paradoxical; they're activists, but they hide behind their computer screens. They're cocky and loud, but they avoid conflict. They want to stand out, but not *too* much – just enough to be cool. They're politically liberal, but they're conservative in their need for direction and stability in their lives. They're idealistic (we can change the world!) but cynical (all ads are lies!). But regardless of the many different faces, one fact is 100% consistent: Gen Y is huge, and they're effecting change, from workplace norms to the music industry all the way to the White House.

People pay top dollar for surveys and insights to help them better understand and leverage this segment, from how to retain them as productive employees to understanding their behavior and attitudes. There are experts galore on how to deal with Gen Y. However, as Walter Cronkite was quoted as saying, **"In seeking truth you have to get both sides of a story."** The story of Gen Y goes beyond statistics and expert speak. In the face of so much media, research, and other forms of attention, analysis, and criticism, what is sometimes overlooked is, well...Gen Y itself. Gen Yers' own voice, insights, and personal opinions on who they are.

The profile that follows is that voice, those insights, those personal opinions – a personal look into the heart of Gen Y.

FIGURE OUT THE TRUTH

WHO WE ARE

MANY CHARACTERS, NOT ONE HERO

Gen Y's story doesn't center around one hero. Instead, multiple characters and multiple faces collectively form the protagonist of this group. Each of these characters, each of these faces, must be recognized to understand the generation as a whole. From Gen Y's political personality to its diverse makeup to its social habits, individuality becomes a defining characteristic of this group.

This generation's need for acceptance and healthy social lives combined with its members' needs to stand out may be the cause for Gen Y's multiple-personality nature. This dual desire results in Gen Y having a multitude of personalities, commitments, and moods that they juggle at once to ensure that they do not miss any opportunity. **Instead of locking themselves into one face and one personality, this group's members wants more, and enjoys the excitement of living dynamic and ever-changing lives.** This generation is still figuring out its identity, and in the meantime, they are trying everything and putting on plenty of different faces. So while they may still be young, they are complex and multi-layered individuals. Gen Y's varying personalities are not always consistent and at times even starkly contrast one another, but the collective result of these many personality pieces is a generation of jam-packed and exciting Gen Y

"I don't think that there is a political party in America that represents my views accurately and fully. I believe in voting for an individual over than a political party."

"I consider myself liberal, though that is mainly because of my beliefs about social issues. My parents insist that once I grow up and have to actually pay taxes and work as a slave to the government for a good chunk of the year, I'll change my mind – or at least mv votes."

lives geared toward finding and capturing fulfillment in every way imaginable.

A PROGRESSIVE GENERATION

One of Gen Y's many distinguishable and central faces is its liberal and socially aggressive look. Indeed, Gen Y is the most liberal generation yet. A New York Times party affiliation study highlights this fact by breaking down who leans toward and affiliates with the two major parties based on respondents' current age. The age level at which the most voters are Democratic is twenty one -

"I consider myself a moderate who usually sides with the Democratic Party in many serious issues. I'd like to claim myself as an Independent, but I side with the Democrats too often. I don't think there is one political party that represents me accurately and fully."

"Nothing represents my views fully, but I associate myself and share the most overlapping views with the Dems. I tend to be pretty liberal on most issues."

right at the heart of Gen Y.[1] The reverse statistic shows that 24-year-olds are the least Republican out of all age groups.

But not only is Gen Y the most liberal generation in current times, it's the most liberal generation at this age of any generation in America's history. The study breaks down affiliation based on those who turned twenty during each administration, from Franklin D. Roosevelt to George W. Bush's first five years. With the older end of Gen Y first eligible to vote in the 2000 and 2004 elections, Gen Y comprises the group of voters who turned twenty during the Bush administration. These voters affiliated with the Democratic Party fifteen percentage points more than the Republican

Party, fifty-two percent to thirty-seven percent. This margin is the largest margin recorded, beating a 13% margin young people showed during the Nixon administration and an 11% margin during the Ford and  Truman administrations. These numbers show that Gen Y is the most Democratic generation in the past seventy years. Indeed, in the 2008 presidential election, a vast majority of young people voted for the Democratic candidate Barack Obama, 66% compared to only 32% for Republican candidate John McCain. This margin is a considerable increase over the 2004 election, where 54% voted for Democratic candidate John Kerry compared to 45% for President George Bush, pointing towards Gen Y's becoming even more liberal as more of its members become eligible to vote. Indeed, between now and 2018, the number of eligible Gen Y voters is expected to increase 4.5 million voters a year.[2]

Other studies similarly point to Gen Y's strongly progressive nature. The Center for American Progress uses a comprehensive 10-item progressive cultural index covering topics from religion, abortion, and homosexuality to race, immigration, and the family, with 10 being the most progressive score and 0 the most conservative. Gen Y scored 56.6 out of 100 on the index, compared to a range of 46.4 to 52.9 for older generations. Furthermore, when broken down into segments, the fastest growing ones are even more progressive – the Hispanic population has grown 32% in the 2000s, and Hispanic Gen Yers score a 61.6 on the progressive cultural index. As progressive minorities continue to grow in size, Gen Y may correspondingly continue down the progressive road.

Political engagement levels are particularly high with college students of Gen Y. In 2008, a record 85.9% of freshman arriving at college reported frequently or occasionally discussing politics in the past year.[3] Of that number, the 35.6% who frequently discussed politics was the highest level of involvement since this particular survey started 43 years prior. This high level of political involvement is particularly impressive in light of the fact that it is higher than the 33.6% who frequently discussed politics in 1968, which most regard as one of the most politically active times among young people, with demonstrations on campuses across the US.

The excitement over the **2008 election is a huge reason for this political involvement, as Gen Yers have a sense of the historical significance of the election: leading up to the election, 75% said it would be the most important or one of the most important in their lifetimes.**[4] Because of this significance, 77% described the campaigns and election as interesting, while only 21% found it dull. Gen Y is thus a politically aware and politically involved generation that understands and relishes in the much-talked-about importance of the young vote.

In President Obama's victory speech in Grant Park, he spoke of how his campaign "grew strength from the young people who rejected the myth of their generation's apathy, who left their homes and families for jobs that offered little pay and less sleep." **The story of President**

Obama's success with this generation reveals much about the way this generation thinks and feels. Obama won the Gen Y vote by communicating the way Gen Y communicates: social networks, grassroots recruiting, and appeals that felt personal and genuine. Obama reached Gen Y through channels they already dominated. He took advantage of the ability to customize technology in a way to reach voters in a never-before-seen personal fashion. No other presidential candidate was sending out personalized text messages to supporters the way Obama did. Obama used this generation's thirst for responsibility and activism and empowered them by handing them the reigns of the campaign. He gave them tools like social networking sites and blogs and let them take control, whether on Twitter, Facebook, or elsewhere.

But Obama's success with Gen Y stretches far beyond his tech-savvy ways. Gen Y gravitated to Obama in large part because he was, put quite simply, "cool." Gen Y grew up hearing stories of John F. Kennedy and his ability to inspire the nation, but no president in Gen Y's lifetime had this aura or inspirational ability. Until President Obama, that is. Obama's passionate and powerful speeches swept Gen Y up, his pleas to be active and be agents of change convinced them, and his star power blew them away. **Obama wasn't just another old, boring candidate. This man watched ESPN, made bracket picks for the NCAA men's basketball tournament, and listened to the Fugees. He was, for the first time in this generation's lifetime, a presidential candidate it**

was not just okay, but genuinely cool, to like. Obama shirts became a fashion symbol, regardless of the fact that the person wearing the shirt might not know a single thing about the president's platform or opinions.

Still other reasons why Obama is so popular may simply be the fact that he *looks* like the future. He's multiracial and identifies himself as black. He's young and "fist-bumps" with his wife on stage. He's new, he's fresh, and, yes, he represents "change." Plenty of Gen Yers genuinely responded to Obama, and plenty of them leapt on that "cool" bandwagon. But by presenting a fresh, exciting, energetic feel to an otherwise stagnant and pessimistic political landscape, Obama was able to reach this group and represent for them a political figure they could connect to and say they support with pride.

Gen Y's liberal tendencies go far beyond one election. As voters' party preferences often develop based on the political atmosphere at the time they come of age, the fact that many Gen Yers became politically aware for the first time during the Clinton administration may have contributed to

"Hands down, the most influential events of my lifetime have been the bombing of the Twin Towers and the Pentagon on September 11th, and Barack Obama's recent rise to the Presidency.

Oh, and the invention of TIVO."

Gen Y's liberal streak. In terms of Gen Y's awareness of politics, a number of key events have taken place during this generation's development that have shaped their political views and enforced a need to be aware and active. The election scandal of 2000 and the ensuing recount brought loads of attention on the election, and while most of this generation was not voting yet, they were able to see firsthand the effect and influence of just a few votes. And while it also may have had a jading effect on the election process and civic duty in general, it brought some much-needed attention to this young group about what makes the election matter and the principles that underlie the process.

A more shocking event that jolted this generation into political awareness is the 9/11 attacks. Such a traumatic event encouraged a number of Gen Y members to pay more attention to political matters. In fact, the number of students who say that keeping up to date with political affairs is an "essential" or "very important" goal was a lowly 28.1% in 2000 but rose to 39.5% in 2008.[5] Gen Y was still young when 9/11 happened, and most of them were probably more concerned with their school outfit on that particular day than with what was going on in the world. But the events of 9/11 forced this generation to deal with, learn about, and talk about extremely serious issues. At the time, Gen Y may not have fully realized the magnitude of what they were experiencing and witnessing, but they certainly the events and the changes in the political climate that ensued certainly affected them. It was a sobering event, but it was an extremely significant learning and growing experience for Gen Y, one that made them truly politically aware for perhaps the first time. Largely because of 9/11, **terrorism has become and will continue to be a subject of constant discussion and extreme**

importance as Gen Y gets older, regardless of political affiliation.

The War on Terror and the Iraq War that ensued after the events of 9/11 have only intensified Gen Y's political stances. **Gen Y's increasing liberal ways can be directly traced to the increasing dismay at the Iraq War.** From the start, the majority of Gen Y was not in favor of invading Iraq, with 58% percent initially opposing the US-led invasion.[6] As the war has progressed, Gen Y has increasingly opposed it, with more than three-fourths of Gen Y strongly opposed the war in 2008, and almost 70% calling for immediate withdrawal of troops.[7] This group came to doubt the Bush administration, as 92% of Gen Yers are not convinced that "weapons of mass destruction" was President Bush's major reason for the war.[8] This further aligned and continues to align Gen Y with the Democratic Party and liberal politics, and the war became an extremely important and highly visible cause around which Gen Y could rally and become active and outspoken.

For the younger end of Gen Y, the War in Iraq is what got them into politics and convinced them to listen to the news and read the paper in the first place.

Sure, most likely a sizable portion of Gen Y just followed the trend and jumped on the "anti-war" bandwagon because it was the young, "cool" thing to do. There are plenty of Gen Yers who oppose the war but do not know the political currents and situations influencing the war itself. For these surface supporters, it could come down to simply wanting to look cool in front of others and fitting in with friends. Taking a stance against the war and speaking out may give off an image of intelligence and intellect. And especially as a young generation, it is easy to jump on that "peace" bandwagon and speak out to support a young generation's ideals. Gen Y is optimistic and idealistic, and its members don't enjoy settling for less. This mindset drives them to stand up for peace. At the same time, they're selfish and want as much as they can get, and this drives them to oppose the war because they'd rather see the government spend those resources on them at home. The fact that the Bush administration became the subject of so many jokes and satires added to Gen Y's opposition to the Iraq War and its support of this "cool" anti-war image. **When TV shows with huge Gen Y audiences like *Saturday Night Live* and *The Daily Show with Jon Stewart* are making fun of President Bush and the administration's stances on the war, Gen Y soaked it all up and laughed right along.** Sure, it's playful humor, but Gen Y responded to it and easily absorbed those humorous stances and their underlying messages. When reciting Jon Stewart's latest witty shots at Bush became "cool," the bandwagon against the Iraq War became that much easier to leap onto, and speaking out against the war became more and more common.

The surface support and bandwagoning works the other way as well. Some Gen Yers mistakenly think Iraq attacked the US on 9/11 or had some sort of direct involvement and that this involvement is the cause of the war. While the debate on the true motives behind the Iraq War rages on, what is clear is that a number of Gen Yers have jumped out in support of the war without true understanding or knowledge of the situation, just like those who jumped out against it. As long as awareness is not 100%, these bandwagoners and misinformed people will continue to be just that, misinformed. But what is most important is that *regardless* of the merits behind the opinions of the war and *regardless* of what is actually motivating these members to speak out against it, the war in itself has made this generation political and has shaped their views and made them public. Talking about the war was the first time many of these Gen Yers truly started talking about politics. The war brought Gen Y to the political table and opened their ears and eyes, and they've been there ever since.

> *"I think there have been many situations where older people have assumed that as a college student I love in a bubble unperturbed and unaware of the world at large – politics, the state of the economy, environmental issues. Not true."*

CARETAKERS AT HOME

Liberal tendencies extend far beyond foreign policy and a single war. Gen Y's political views focus strongly on domestic issues including the environment and poverty and social issues like abortion and gay marriage. And, with the onset of the economic crisis effecting Gen Y in numerous, important, and lasting ways, the economy has risen to the top of the list of issues Gen Y cares about and wants addressed.

"I recycle whatever I can, and I try not to waste any resources that don't need wasting – but that's not enough. Plus, I really only turn off my bathroom light because I don't want to pay the bill."

When it comes to the environment, Gen Y is Gen Green. According to a 2008

Peanut Labs study of 1,070 Gen Y respondents, the environment was one topic on which Gen Y was extremely unified, with 80.5% of respondents in favor of legislation to reduce greenhouse gas emissions and 89.5% supporting the development of alternative fuels.[9] This generation has grown up hearing so much about America's dependence on foreign

"I am much more likely to purchase from a company that is socially responsible."

"I think that the environment is important to take care of, but most of the green trend is just keeping up with the Joneses or just using it as an excuse to cut back on expenses."

oil that unlike previous generations, they grew up with a heightened sense of the necessity of alternative fuels and new energy ideas. Combine this mindset with the budget of a young generation and the high prices of gas, and this group is all in favor of new ideas and better options. Again, while Gen Y may not know the driving forces behind oil prices and the energy industry, they do know that new energy ideas and fuels are "cool" and progressive, and that resonates with them.

Gen Y has grown up familiar with the recent "green" movement. They know no different, and as a result, **they have come to view these environmentally friendly measures not as drastic changes but almost as an expectation.** A full 84% of Gen Yers are actively concerned about the climate crisis to the extent that it significantly affects their career choices.[10] Eighty-one percent of Gen Yers say it is important to work for a green company, and seventy-nine percent say they are more likely to accept a job offer at a green company when considering two options. Only 16% currently work or intern at a green company, however, so the opportunity for improvement is readily apparent. These Gen Yers are settling for less when they aren't working for a "green" company, and they're certainly not going to be happy with settling for less. They expect and demand "green," and they care enough to drive the change to make "green" changes happen.

This group is not satisfied with how active they are about the green movement, either. Twenty percent of Gen Yers say they need more green products to choose from, and nineteen percent want more education about actions they can take to help. Given how such a large part of Gen Y is still getting some form of education, these numbers speak to both the opportunities available and to the level of importance the environment holds with this group that they want to learn more about this subject on top of all the others they are already studying. And what's at stake? When it comes to the environment, Gen Y is more than just talk. **Nearly half of Gen Y is willing to pay more for environmentally safe products, services, or brands.** [11] Gen Y's environmental attitudes are more than just complaining or posturing. They care, and their actions show it.

We only have one planet and it's our collective individual responsibility to take care of it. If every person changes their wasteful habits, there will be an effect."

"We must all care for the environment for today's generation and all future generations. I made my parents trade our gas guzzling SUVs and minivans for fuel efficient compact cars."

My one bottle of Windex isn't causing global warming."

Gen Y's liberal streak stretches beyond just the environment and tackles social issues like abortion and gay marriage. While abortion continues to be a polarizing issue, with both Gen Y and the general population split and often extremely passionate about their views, recent surveys show Gen Y clearly is "pro-choice." In a 2008 American University online survey of 18-29 year olds, 49% of respondents identified themselves as "pro-choice," while only 29% identified as "pro-life" and 21% as "somewhere in between."[12]

Some Gen Yers may be in support of a woman's right to an abortion because they disagree with the religious motivation of social views, as 64% in one youth survey say "religious faith should focus more on promoting tolerance, social justice, and peace and less on opposing abortion or gay rights."[13] Gen Y's majority belief in a woman's right to have an abortion leads to Gen Y's more general views of gender equality and gender roles. As the divorce rate increases and family structures change, **many Gen Yers have grown up in nontraditional environments.** Married couples with children account for fewer than one fourth of all households, while in 1960 married couples with children were a full one-half of all households.[14] Additionally, 53% of all married couples in 1972 fit the definition of a traditional family, where the husband works and the wife stays home. Today, just 26% fit that definition, while the proportion of married couples who both work outside the home has risen to 52% from 32% in 1972.

All these trends in changing family structures and gender roles has led to Gen Y leading the charge in expecting equality for women. In 2008, when asked whether women's role was "in the home" or "having an equal role with men in running business, industry, and government," 90% of Gen Yers strongly supported an equal role with men, which was the highest of any generation polled.[15] These figures show that Gen Y strongly support gender equality.

Gay marriage is another issue that shows a clear divide, a divide that religious beliefs unsurprisingly determine largely. However, while this issue is also a hotly debated and polarizing one, recent surveys show Gen Y is leading the charge to legalize gay marriage. May Gallup data showed 59% support for legalizing gay marriage among 18- to 29-year-old Gen Yers, compared to only 40% support among 30- to 49-year-olds and 37% support among 50- to 64-year-olds.[16] Gen Y and younger people's liberal stance on this issue compared to older

generations is shown in a recent CNN poll, which found that 58% of 18-34 year olds said same-sex marriage should be legal, compared to only 42% of those age 35-49 and 41% of those age 50-64.[17] An April *Washington Post*/ABC News poll found even higher support among Gen Y, with 66% of 18- to 29-year-olds supporting legalizing gay marriage.[18] While the nation as a whole is split on this issue, these figures show that the youngest voters are the ones most strongly in favor of marriage equality. Even on the nation's most polarizing issues, **Gen Y leans toward the**

liberal and progressive views that support a woman's right to an abortion and the right to same-sex marriage.

The fact that Gen Y leans in support of same-sex marriage is not entirely surprising, because although religious affiliation determines many views on this issue, Gen Y's overall views on diversity and equality have grown to encompass not just race and gender but sexual orientation, as well. This generation is less traditional, and the majority of them do not understand why a gay person would not get the same rights to marriage as anyone else.

When it comes to healthcare and new government programs, Gen Y is definitively progressive, as well. According to a 2008 Center for American Progress report, this generation is "more likely to support universal health coverage than any age group in the thirty previous years the question has been asked."[19] An impressive 57% of 18-29-year-olds responded that health insurance should come from a government insurance plan. Critics argue that this idealism on healthcare is because much of this generation is still ignorant of the burden of taxes, but as Gen Yers continue to enter adulthood, they have not yet wavered. Indeed, an overwhelming 87% of Gen Yers "think the government should spend more money on health care even if a tax increase is required to pay for it." This is the highest level of support in the question's 20-year history, revealing Gen Y as the most progressive group in recent history concerning healthcare.

Gen Y not only wants more invested in programs like universal healthcare, they want new programs offered by the government. **Sixty-one percent of Gen Yers "think the government should provide more services," which is the highest response of any age group in the twenty years the question was asked.**[20] When it comes to producing jobs, Gen Y expects a lot of the government as well. Forty-five percent of Gen Yers said that the government should see to a good job and standard of living for everyone, compared to thirty-two percent of 30-59-year-olds. Gen Y expects a lot from the government, and wants to see the benefits the government has to offer.

"I guess I would be a liberal. I am pro-choice, pro-gay marriage, pro stem cell research, not very religious."

"I am politically complicated. I don't think that any party has everything right, and I base my views on separate issues off of my own personal convictions rather than just subscribing to one party's platform."

Again, some of this optimism about investing strongly in the government and starting new programs could stem from Gen Y's relative idealism and young age. They are still young and have high expectations. Why *wouldn't* a young, optimistic group want the government to supply steady jobs, good healthcare, new, beneficial programs, and more? Taxes are still a hard concept for younger members of this generation to grasp, and time will tell how this generation's views might change as they age more and pay more taxes. At least for now, they seem to be willing to make the investment.

Additionally, as a young group, this generation is in a position where they *need* government help. While 96% of senior citizens have health insurance, only 63% of Gen Yers do, so of course they would want the government to supply it for them.[21] Moreover, as companies continue to cut back on benefits, the support for government help might only continue to increase. Sure, this generation is thirsty to earn their living, but they are still needy and are still coddled, and consequently expect the government to fulfill those needs and coddle them a bit, too.

> *"I would consider myself Catholic and relatively conservative in my values but secular and progressive with regards to political issues, such as stem cell research. For instance, as a student of the University of Norte Dame, I welcome Obama coming to receive an honorary degree but oppose the media's support of premarital sex and watching distasteful reality TV shows."*

Another reason why Gen Y so strongly supports government action is the fact that they still have relatively high confidence in that government. Critics and doubters call this generation apathetic, but statistics show that this generation still thinks government can work. In 1987, when asked if people agree with the statement, "When something is run by the federal government it is usually ineffective and wasteful," 54% of people 18-29 agreed, compared to 69% of those 30-59 years old. Ten years later, only 42% of 18-29-year-olds agreed, while the number of 30-59-year-olds who agreed stayed high, at 70%.[22] Clearly, Gen Y still believes the government can be beneficial and effective. And while the recent economic crisis and worsening job market may test this generation's confidence in government and their beliefs that government can be effective, it may also push this group even harder to support government help and reform. So even while the economic climate worsens and government is getting plenty of blame, Gen Y's strong liberal stances on such a broad array of subjects suggests this generation will stay on this progressive and aggressive track.

One compelling aspect of Gen Y's progressive nature is the role religion plays. Unaffiliated or secular voters are strongly progressive on cultural issues, scoring a 63.7 on the progressive cultural index, above even the 56.6 of all Gen Y.[23] The percentage of adults reporting no religious affiliation has almost tripled from 1944 to 2004, and projections show that by 2024, 20% of adults will be unaffiliated. This, combined with the projection that less than half of adults will be white Christians by 2024, points to the possibility that as more of the population and more of Gen Y become less religious, more progressive views will increasingly prevail.

From foreign policy to the environment to healthcare and abortion, Gen Y is liberal on a number of key political issues. This group's dislike of the Bush administration and admiration for the new Obama administration further solidifies Gen Y's liberal tendencies. This generation grew up in a tumultuous atmosphere of national disasters like Hurricane Katrina, foreign conflicts like the wars in Iraq and Afghanistan, and emerging global powers and new global dynamics. This context has led Gen Y to expect and demand plenty from the government, and to be politically aware while remaining determinedly idealistic. And while plenty of members of Gen Y are surface supporters of political causes and simply jump on the latest political bandwagon and adopt the latest political "cool" trendy stance, plenty of others earnestly care and are very aware.

Regardless of whether the motivation is a cool Obama t-shirt or a strong personal belief about the environment or the war, this generation has been pushed to be politically aware and active, and they will continue to make their voices heard on all of these issues, expressing their progressive stances. Gen Y's strong stances on certain political issues reveals that, while this is an individualistic and "me" generation, this group can also be collectivist and sacrifice some individual benefits for the benefit of the group. This group is unique and has learned to value individualism and collectivism at the same time. They are determined to change the political landscape and leave their stamp on American and global politics for good.

MULTICULTURAL CITIZENS

Fundamentally intertwined with Generation Y's liberal tendencies is their tremendous diversity, a diversity that is formidable and highly influential in defining and characterizing this group. Gen Y is the most ethnically diverse generation in America, with only 60% identifying as Caucasian.[24] The 40% minority are 18% Hispanic, 14% black, 5% Asian, and 3% other. This minority is only continuing to grow, so quickly in fact that the latest U.S. Census projections point to a minority majority as early as 2042. For the population under the age of 18, that tipping point date moves as early as 2023.[25] Because of this ethnic diversity, this group is comfortable surrounding themselves with people from various and different backgrounds, whether it is religious affiliation or race. In a recent survey done by Rebooters.net, only 7% of respondents said their friends were all the same race or religion.[26]

Gen Yers have grown up in more diverse settings than ever, and it shows in their individual networks. Gen Y's comfort level with diverse peoples also shows itself in this group's opinions on immigration, as this generation more heavily supports immigration and views it as strengthening American society when compared to the more traditional views of older generations. Seventy-three percent of Gen Yers support giving illegal immigrants "the right to live here legally if they pay a fine and meet other requirements" compared to only 42% of seniors agreeing with this statement.[27] Gen Y's comfort level with diversity and differences is only strengthened by this young group's desire to travel and experience new cultures and fresh environments. What is different and what is new is exciting, and Gen Y will chase that excitement and embrace it. Traditional comfort zones are mundane in comparison and don't satisfy anymore. Diversity is interesting, and interesting grabs attention and is what Gen Y craves.

"Diversity is important to me in that it encourages empathy and contributes to our development."

"I try to involve myself in as many organizations and groups as possible, so I have friends from almost every possible backaround."

As a young group used to diversity and non-traditional lifestyles in their classrooms and communities, Gen Y knows no different and expects, embraces, and even takes for granted this diversity everywhere its members go. This fundamental change in how diversity and race in particular is perceived can be attributed in part to the increase of interracial dating and marriages, as Gen Yers are no doubt more familiar and comfortable with having family members of other racial and ethnic backgrounds. An overwhelming 94% of Gen Yers accept the idea of interracial dating and marriage; in contrast, in 1987-88, just 56% of 18- to 25-year olds agreed with this idea.[28] Additionally, 67% of 18- to 25-year-old Gen Yers thought the growing number of immigrants strengthens American society, a much stronger positive sentiment than any other generation showed. The consequence of this increase in interracial relationships is more prevalent acceptance of others. There are more and more multiracial Americans who do not fit into the traditional and stereotypical "categories" that may have been more accepted in the past, and Gen Yers reject racial conflict in favor of collaboration and acceptance. **The continued blending of peoples and cultures does not mean that Gen Y is "color-blind," and that younger Americans no longer see race.** It is still very much a part of their lives, with pop culture and media shaping much of Gen Y's perception of diversity and racial issues.

Many Gen Y members may perceive themselves as crossing color lines simply through consumerism and cultural tourism. And while watching hip-hop videos on MTV may not exactly equate to profound understanding, for some Gen Yers, music videos, commercials, or TV shows significantly shape their understanding of race. While traditional lines are changing, the result of Gen Y's consumerist nature can also lead to a situation where race is misunderstood or trivialized. Being comfortable speaking openly does not always equate to having a true understanding, and race and diversity will continue to be a subject that matters and influences this generation.

Much like with Gen Y's politics, this surface level understanding of race may mean that the level at which Gen Y *thinks* it understands and celebrates diversity is different from the level at which Gen Y *actually*

> *"I don't think diversity necessarily has to refer to race. I think things like coming from different areas of the country, having different family lifestyles, participating in different activities, and having different life goals can make a group of friends diverse. Diversity is important to me because life would get boring if the people that you surround yourself with were all the same, it's great to learn things from others who have a different background than you do. My group of friends is diverse in many ways, but we also have things in common that bring us together."*

exists. **Gen Y has grown up in such a politically correct culture that celebrating diversity is just one of those givens in society.** For some, diversity may simply be one of those "cool" things that you're "supposed" to believe in. For others, multiculturalism is more about being unique than it is about celebrating cultures. Someone may get a trendy Chinese symbol tattoo, but that doesn't mean for a second that he cares about the culture. Still, what is clear is that the vast majority of Gen Y *believes* they are extremely tolerant and understanding. The 2008 CIRP Freshman Survey shows that Gen Y consistently rates itself as having more skills for a diverse workplace compared to their peers. Seventy-nine percent of freshmen believe they are in the "Top 10%" or "Above average" compared to peers for the "ability to work cooperatively with diverse people," and 72.3% believe they are in the "Top 10%" or "Above average" in terms of "tolerance of others with different beliefs."[29] In terms of "Ability to see the world from someone else's perspective," 65.4% of freshmen place themselves above their peers. So, while these responses are only self-perception, and while these figures pertain only to 2008 freshman and not all of Generation Y, it is noteworthy that there is a prevalent feeling of confidence among young people today that they are comfortable and confident with diversity and diverse settings, and that they are understanding and tolerant. This viewpoint is one that, accurate or not, Gen Y takes pride in and even brags about. It is an extremely important way that this generation defines itself.

As Gen Y talks about this subject more and expects more ethnic and racial diversity, it is noteworthy that this group's very definition of diversity is changing beyond the realms of race and religion to include diversity of sexual orientation, family structures, and other alternative lifestyles as well. **More and more young people are choosing to define themselves less by race or ethnicity and more**

by lifestyle, community, and common interests - it's becoming less about being white or black, and more about being a hipster, a Brooklyn kid, or a hip-hop fan. This generation's full impact may significantly alter and expand the light in which people look at diversity and civil rights. As Gen Yers continue to figure out how race and diversity play a role in their own lives, this subject will continue to be a part of their collective definition, whether through the acceptance of race and diversity as a defining feature or the rejection of it as relevant in today's age.

As Gen Y has more diverse and different faces than ever before, these faces are going to school more than ever and living increasingly different and complex lifestyles. With the importance of school instilled in many Gen Y members from their Baby Boomer parents, Gen Yers show their dual personality nature in their work hard, play hard mentality of being serious students and also extremely social partiers. **Gen Yers believe they can study and work for the future without sacrificing a moment of living in the present.**

SCHOOL-LOVERS

Because much of this generation's Baby Boomer parents were successful and raised their Gen Y kids in comfortable settings, Gen Yers are going to and staying in school more than ever before.

Going to college is becoming less of a crowning achievement or a bonus and more of an expectation fostered since these Gen Yers were learning their ABCs.

The number of Gen Y undergraduates qualified for college will increase by 19% between 1995 and 2015, an increase of 2.6 million students. Furthermore, a whopping 80% of this increase will be minority students. Gen Y parents raised this group with the importance of a good education ingrained in them from a young age,

"I have always been pretty gung-ho about my academia, most likely because that was the general attitude of my family growing up. I did my work, was generally prepared (or over prepared) for exams, and never skipped class. My parent's views [on academics] are not only important to me, but they have molded my own ambitions, so much that these days I hold a higher standard for myself than they do."

and it shows in Gen Y's serious approach to school and going to college to set up for a good career and make money. With global competition ever increasing and an increasingly competitive job market, Gen Y is starting to realize the importance of going to college and doing well to keep up with quickening pace of competition. Gen Y knows how to get serious and get work done when necessary. And with more school options than ever before, the environment is ripe for these Gen Yers to have the chance to prove themselves, whether it's a 4-year university or college, vocational school, technical college, community college, online college, or other options. Additionally, as more friends go off to college and experience that lifestyle, more members of Gen Y will want to stay with those friends and share those experiences.

"Academics are my top priority now. I'm a little tougher on myself when it comes to grades than my parents are."

A result of Generation Y growing up in a hypercompetitive arena is that this group has learned to thrive in competition; they are not easily intimidated. By knowing no other situation but one in which students compete with tens, hundreds, and thousands of others for those coveted A's on the résumé and the flashiest jobs in the market, these Gen Yers are confident and self-assured in how they stack up against the rest. Competition may be a reason to complain, but it's something this group is familiar with and it's a major force driving this group's ambitions and self-confidence.

As the vast majority of Gen Yers have experienced, are experiencing, or will experience college life, and as they hear all about it from their wide network of friends in college, their expectations and demands for a college education and lifestyle are changing to fit with their other core characteristics. Gen Y grew up coddled by parents and showered with affection. **They are used to attention, and lots of it.** In college settings, this translates to Gen Y demanding immediate feedback and immediate responses at all times. Sending a professor an email at three in the morning is perfectly normal for this group. They expect constant availability, whether its online office hours with a professor in a chat room or course conferences where students can find out information 24/7. As Gen Y lives such chaotic and fragmented lives, they expect their schools to accommodate this lifestyle. Libraries had better be open 24/7 for Gen Y to do their homework at 4:00 a.m. in the morning. Cafés had better stay open late so students can get that 3:00 a.m. latte. College all-nighters are by no means a new phenomenon, but demanding the library be well-lit and open at 5am, with two flat-screen computer monitors at each desk to do work and email at the same time, with a café inside that's open 24/7 – well, the all-nighter is a bit modified now. This is a generation of open information and instant gratification, and they're taking that culture with them to college and are transforming college life. Gone are the days when students are afraid of professors and when they keep to themselves. College students today unabashedly reach out to professors and expect them to be available. They value the interaction and want to feel like someone is always there to help. So whether it's a professor answering emails at midnight the night before an exam, or telling students to text message him with questions, professor-student relationships are changing to reflect Gen Y's lifestyle and characteristics.

"Academics and schoolwork are the foundations for a better future. My parents have drilled this believe into my head and now I live by it."

Recently, the economic downturn has affected the Gen Y college student both positively and negatively. Seventy-five percent of Gen Yers are worried about paying for college given the current economic climate, and of those seventy-five percent, a third are "very worried."[30] This concern has lead to 13% dropping some courses, 5% moving back in with parents, and 33% taking on a part-time job or a second job in addition to their studies. Gen Y is being forced to realize that the ideal, romanticized party lifestyle at college is not a given, and with financial pressures, they have to deal with making some sacrifices. While Gen Y college students are making some tough choices, they also are looking on the bright side of the situation: 86% feel college is the best investment they can make, and a whopping 96% said "yes" when asked, "In times of economic crisis, does a college degree become even more important for your employability?" **While the economic downturn has real consequences for the Gen Y college student and their lifestyle, these students are also optimistic and view college as a valuable resource that will pay off in the future.** Given this attitude, Gen Y students are not going to stop flocking to college anytime soon.

SOCIALITES

But make no mistake, Gen Y isn't about to be classified simply as ambitious students and the rising doctors, lawyers, and politicians of the world. This group's ambitions go far beyond books, and their social personality comes out the second those books close, if they can even wait that long. While Gen Yers understand the need to do well in school, they consider being social and having a good time a big priority, too. With wide networks and a desire to be noticed and remembered, this group goes out often and makes sure they're not wasting the years and opportunities of their youth. Gen Yers tend to enjoy socializing and meeting new people, and they enjoy widening that network of people who know them. **The bigger the better when it comes to the networks of people who one can influence.** Additionally, with means of social communication more convenient and prevalent than ever before, **no Gen Yer is ever separated from friends and social happenings,** making it easier than ever before to stay connected with what's going on and what the next party's going to be. Friends can hear about the next big party through a Facebook event and invite all their friends in an instant. They can log in the day before the party and see who is going to decide whether it's cool enough for them to attend.

"I like Facebook because it is a great way to organize social events and stay connected with friends I don't see on a regular basis."

Connection with those wide networks is constant, and Gen Y takes that connection for granted to the extent that the second a Gen Yer is cut off from

the social network of friends, panic will no doubt ensue. This group is impatient, with high social expectations, and

sitting at home when one could be out having experiences that are more social is simply unacceptable.

VOLUNTEERS

Gen Y's social nature contributes to and works well with Gen Y's civic-minded nature. Surveys show that Gen Y is "the most civic-minded since the generation of the 1930s and 1940s."[31] This may be a generation that enjoys attention, but from day one, parents and educators have ingrained in Gen Y the value of volunteering and helping others.

Gen Y has incorporated civic duty into its identity. Hurricane Katrina was a defining moment for this generation, and natural disasters like Katrina and tragedies like 9/11 brought the very real need for helping others to the forefront for Gen Y. This group saw natural disasters at home and wars fought abroad, and growing up in that situation pressed Gen Y to realize the need to pull together and work together. Combine Gen Y's

"I usually [volunteer] for the free t-shirt. That's why those big events are the best. You always get a bright blue t-shirt that says "Volunteer" on the back. I never really wear them outside of the event, but it's always nice to have!"

"Family and service to society is important to me. I think we ought to love one another and show it. I care about poverty reduction and education. I also feel we may have lost the sense of personal responsibility our grandparents' held. If I had it my way, people would actually feel guilty for sitting around playing World of Warcraft all day instead of out doing something for others."

recognition of this need to help others with its optimistic and activist nature, and the result is a generation that loves to volunteer and help others, a generation that believes it can make a positive change.

A closer look shows how volunteering actually fits quite nicely with some of Gen Y's other core characteristics. Helping others and being knowledgeable about what's going on in the world, whether through donations or volunteering, are ways that Gen Y can stand out, get attention, and have experiences that they can share with others. The internet has connected Gen Y with the world, and it has bred a culture where Gen Y can fight genocide in Darfur with the click of a mouse on Facebook or donate a pound of rice to children in Africa by joining a group on MySpace. Gen Y enjoys feeling connected with the world, and these charitable and volunteer causes are ways in which Gen Y can express that connection. While joining a Facebook group to fight genocide is hardly being an activist, the internet brings issues to Gen Y's doorstep and helps get them involved.

Gen Y's global nature also contributes to Gen Ys' civic-minded nature because it gives them an opportunity to experience the world, not just connect to it online.

This generation loves to travel and studies abroad in huge numbers.

Volunteering is one way in which Gen Y can travel and experience the world. Whether it means joining international groups that work in a variety of countries or getting a scholarship to do charity work abroad, volunteering is a fast way for Gen Y to travel the world and gain new, fulfilling experiences.

As Gen Y flocks to those new, fulfilling experiences, its members also share them unabashedly with others. Volunteering is a social act, and whether it's helping others with friends and family or writing about a volunteer mission on a Facebook note or blog page, volunteering and helping others gives Gen Y something to talk about and share, a fulfilling experience that gives Gen Y a good feeling of making a difference in others' lives.

"I have learned that I should only volunteer with activities that I am interested in; otherwise I don't feel that I've used my time well."

New social networking sites are popping up that capitalize on the social approach Gen Y has to volunteer work. New sites like ActofGood.org are social networking sites that connect volunteers and charities and offer discussion and education opportunities. **These sites realize that Gen Y love to volunteer and *really* love to talk about it,** and connecting volunteers with others and helping spread those just causes and opportunities will only increase the number of Gen Y volunteers who are out there helping others and sharing their stories.

While volunteering is an opportunity for Gen Y to affect others and share memorable experiences, it is also, simply put, practical. **Schools force community service down students' throats at an early age, stressing the importance of having a well-rounded resume.**

Where schools and leaders don't require volunteering of students, they certainly strongly recommend it. Schools and communities give students plenty of opportunities to volunteer, and it has become a norm for students and a part of their lifestyle. Companies and colleges like seeing those service experiences and community involvement, and Gen Y knows that. It serves them well to serve others, and as long as that holds, students will continue to volunteer in huge numbers, if only to help their chances of getting into that Ivy League school.

The last couple of years in particular have seen more and more volunteering opportunities and activities for Gen Y. More and more colleges are capitalizing on Gen Y's desires to volunteer by offering "alternative spring breaks," where students can pass on partying in Cancun to travel to the Gulf Coast and volunteer to help reconstruct areas damaged by the hurricanes of 2005. The

"I don't regularly volunteer, mainly because I'm focused on activities that will get me to my next stage in life. Sadly, until school is over, the primary motivating factor behind doing anything besides the basics is to ultimately impress the next school, the next opportunity to win an award, or a future boss. Right now, my volunteering isn't going to impress anyone. Pathetic? Sure. Heartless? Unfortunately."

United Way started setting up campus chapters in 2008, a sign that other service organizations are hoping to capitalize on the Gen Y college students' willingness to volunteer.

The latest influence on Gen Y and volunteering has been President Obama's campaign and ascent to office. A former community organizer himself, Obama repeatedly called on young people to be active, and called on everyone but especially young voters to serve their communities and be active to help improve the nation. Gen Y responded to Obama's call and rallied around him. Time will tell if his call to service will have a lasting effect on this generation or if it was merely a short-term response, but in the days surrounding Obama's inauguration, online applications to the Peace Corps spiked 175%.[32]

Recent economic woes are even more reason for Gen Y to volunteer. In such a terrible job market, volunteering becomes a great alternative to getting a job.

Service organizations are seeing tremendous spikes in numbers, as more and more Gen Y members are giving up on the job search and turning to service organizations as an alternative career move. As fewer are recruiting on campuses, more and more service organizations like Teach for America are increasing their on-campus presence to capitalize on the situation. Nearly 25,000 students applied for Teach for America, a 37% increase over 2007 figures.[33] City Year, which offers volunteers monthly stipends, had tripled the number of applications in the past year. Whether Gen Y is volunteering to travel the world, to substitute for a job, or to have fulfilling experiences, volunteer numbers are continuing to increase.

Volunteering is a form of empowerment for this generation, a way to influence others in a positive way while improving oneself at the same time. While Obama's inspiring call to service and a down economy are contributing significantly to these increased volunteer numbers, the volunteering face of Gen Y has always been there. It fits with Gen Y's social nature, desire to influence, and thirst for new experiences, and it is a trend that shows no sign of slowing down.

LOOKING AHEAD

What are the results of these many faces, this frenetic pace, and the often-schizophrenic nature of Generation Y? Effective segmentation becomes harder, and traditional demographics are becoming less and less effective. Gen Y is constantly changing identities and personalities; they like options and variety. Additionally, the amount of clutter and noise in Gen Y's lives continues to increase, and breaking through becomes a daunting challenge.

SHORT STORIES

Generation Y's story is comprised of countless short stories. This generation refuses to settle for following one central path. Instead, its members enjoy a vast array of short, exciting stories, any number of which are beginning or ending at any given time. The result is a unique and exciting mosaic of every type of story imaginable, all occurring at once to complete the overarching Gen Y tale.

The members of Generation Y are young, and they are restless. One central story would bore this group to death. To ensure that their lives stay exciting and new, this generation has developed to be masters of movement.

MULTITASKERS

Gen Y's lives are fragmented and frenetic, but they are master multitaskers with short attention spans who love and need these various plotlines to fully satisfy their expansive needs and desires.

A product of Gen Y wanting it all is that they can be a student one minute and a partier the next. **These lifestyles overlap to the point where it's completely ordinary for a student to be studying in the library while texting friends and Facebook chatting others to hype up a party later that night, all while studying in a circle of friends who are talking about biology and gossip in the same conversation.**

"Currently, I'm not only talking about multi-tasking, but also listening to music, and putting together a report for my boss... all while sipping on a Diet Coke. I can multi-task in almost any situation. It's easy to do with computers and cell phones. Hold up, my cell phone is vibrating... another thing to add to my multitask list!"

Recent innovations and technologies have driven the creation and adoption of this new lifestyle that Gen Y has so energetically and effortlessly embraced. Why watch TV when one can watch TV and surf the net on a laptop at the same time? Why waste time when one can email, call, text, and play games on one phone on the way to class? The multitasking nature of new devices and technologies has translated into a multitasking nature in Gen Y, one that reaches beyond technology and entertainment to all corners of life.

Growing up with multiple forms of entertainment available at once and widespread instant gratification has led to this generation having higher levels of expectations and higher criteria for satisfaction. It takes more to impress Gen Y, more to entertain them, more to grab their attention, and even more to keep it. Gen Yers have multiple conversations at once with multiple people in multiple places. At school, they're juggling classes, clubs, sports, and other extracurricular activities without blinking an eye. At home, they're texting, calling, instant messaging, social networking, and eating at the same time, all while lying down on the couch.

"Multitasking is my life's fuel. I get bored with complacency so I make sure to keep myself involved in anything of interest. There's no other way to survive a day in my shoes without multi-tasking."

Take the average student's typical evening. In the past, the student might come home from school, grab a snack, sit down in her room and do problem sets of homework for a few hours. Then she'd have dinner with the family, sit down, and enjoy some TV. How does that typical evening look now? That student will come home, snack while talking on the phone with her friend, lie down on the couch with her laptop, turn on the TV, open iTunes, blast some music, instant message her friends, sign on to Facebook, and work on her problem set during the brief gaps where her instant message chats are quiet and a commercial break is on TV. It might not be the most efficient way to do work, but it is how this generation gets it done.

Even *in* school, more and more students use their laptops and multimedia phones to chat with friends and surf the web during class. Call it rude, but parents and other influential people spoiled this generation to the point where they demand constant entertainment, even in the classroom. If the professor's not showing them YouTube videos, bet on the fact that they're watching them themselves on their phones or computers.

Take any one of the millions of options of entertainment and experiences that these Gen Yers have available to them, and this group will notice something's missing and expect something new and exciting to fill the gap. So, while pinpointing what Gen Y is doing at any given time is uncertain to say the least, what is certain is that this group is extremely tough to overwhelm and is comfortable and confident handling a whole lot on their plates at once.

It may be questionable whether that comfort level and confidence with multitasking actually translates into positive results. But in the end, it doesn't matter to this generation. In the case of the student, it might take her an hour longer to do her problem set than if she sat down with no outside influences and just worked. But what torture that would be! So while Gen Y's parents kept yelling to turn off the music while doing work, this generation craves the stimulus and needs to balance work with play.

But Gen Y's multitasking tendencies extend far beyond school and homework. As more and more Gen Yers enter the workplace, they bring their multitasking nature with them. In a survey of white collar and legal professionals, when asked to report how many total hours each day they spend accessing various devices, **Gen Y respondents reported spending 17.4 hours a day using a personal computer, PDA or Blackberry, and mobile phone** (8.5 on computer, 4.0 on PDA, and 4.9 on mobile phone).[34] In contrast, the total hours spent by Baby Boomers was 9.7 hours per day. On a similar question, when asked how many total hours a day they spend using different computer applications, Gen Y respondents spent 20.5 hours a day using email and calendar programs, internet browsers, instant messaging programs, and Microsoft Office (5.4 on email/calendar, 6.9 on internet browser, 3.1 on IM, and 5.1 on Microsoft Office). Baby Boomers spent only 11.9 hours a day on these applications, in contrast. Assuming Gen Y

"I usually tend to procrastinate instead of multitasking. I focus on one project but take breaks to talk to friends, eat, or relax, then come back to my work re-energized and ready to focus."

professionals aren't working 18-21 hour workdays, it's safe to say these numbers show that Gen Y workers multitask at higher levels in the workplace, using multiple devices and technologies at once to get things done. Time spent on one application like IM is overlapped with time spent on a calendar and time spent with Microsoft Excel open at the same time. On top of all that, expect Gen Y to be multitasking by playing music, as well, with 84% of these Gen Y respondents saying they found it very or somewhat acceptable to listen to an online radio station at work. In contrast, only 63% of Baby Boomers felt the same way. And while all workers these days may have Microsoft Outlook and Internet Explorer open while working on a PDA and might enjoy a good tune, these figures show Gen Y use these applications and devices almost twice as much as their older Baby Boomer counterparts. While this survey is limited to white collar and legal professionals, who may be more dependent on these applications in their professions, it is a useful example that Gen Yers are taking multitasking to a new level in the workplace, juggling all of their options and tools simultaneously and using their familiarity with the technology to handle the load. They not only can handle the multitasking way of doing things, they *rely* on it. Why just do work when one can do work while listening to music and instant messaging? This generation is not overwhelmed entering the workplace; they use their multitasking nature to get things done, in a way they want it done.

It's a classic case of the chicken or the egg, but Gen Y's shortened attention span is intertwined with this group's avid use of multiple forms of entertainment and devices. This is very much an ADD generation. If Gen Y is not completely entertained, they'll immediately stop what they're doing to find a better option. Gen Y's tastes can be fickle and their trends can catch on in an instant, and the result is that Gen Y's attention is not only fragmented but is focused on any one subject for shorter and shorter periods of time. What else could be expected?

Generation Y grew up living comfortably, and many Baby Boomer helicopter parents spoiled and coddled their Gen Y kids. And while the constant hovering no doubt led and continues to lead to the eternal eye roll of youth, it also created an expectation of constant satisfaction, of getting what Gen y wants, when Gen Y wants it. The sheer amount of attention devoted to this generation from such a young age means they are used to the spotlight and expect people to be reward them at every turn. In addition to the coddling, this group has grown up bombarded with fast-action television shows and action movies, providing a constant stimulus and a blanket of entertainment, a literal wall of noise and explosions that Gen Y soaked in with wide eyes and dropped jaws. This fast-action childhood has trained this group to find silence and waiting simply unacceptable. Gen Y likes and demands new and interesting things in their lives at all times, and by constantly mixing up what their focus is on, they can keep their lives fresh. The result of this obsession with keeping things fresh? Gen Yers may very well start projects and activities they never finish, get bored with activities that were their favorite the day before, and have other sudden changes in mood and perceptions without ever looking back.

SPEED DEMONS

Complementing Gen Y's multitasking nature is the blinding speed at which this generation lives its lives. Make no mistake – it's all about speed.

The environment in which this generation grew up sheds light on why this group is as restless as they are. This group grew up in an age of technology and ever-increasing efficiency. Everything, *everything*, became faster. Mailing a letter used to take at least a few days. But with email and text messaging? Communication became instantaneous. Buying music and movies used to take a drive to the store, a wait in the checkout line, and a drive back home. Now, users can go online and download them in a matter of seconds. The enjoyment is immediate. America's culture is one of efficiency and instant gratification, and the remarkable advancements in just the past fifteen years have drastically improved that efficiency and speed of gratification. Technology is obviously a gigantic driver of these improvements, and it is with technology that this generation grew up. The result is clear: this generation knows no alternative to the instant gratification that technology provides, and activities that used to take time now take much less. Put simply, this generation does not know how to *wait*. When Gen Y wants something, they want it now.

Growing up in this age means Gen Y takes speed and instant gratification for granted. They expect it, they demand it, and they whine without it. If they can't enjoy something immediately, they do not have the patience to wait for a very long time, and instead will find something else to do that will gratify them immediately. This impatience, this restlessness, means Generation Y is constantly looking for something to occupy and entertain them, and if it can't deliver immediately, they will continue the search for something that can.

TREND JUMPERS

One result of this restlessness is that Gen Y jumps from trend to trend extremely quickly. They are fast to adopt a new trend, and even faster to drop it for a newer, shinier one. This generation is in constant communication and its social nature extends to broader networks of friends and family. What is popular today does not take nearly as long to spread through word of mouth as it did fifty years ago. Generation Y's members are masters of the rumor, the whisper, the story, and if they find a new product or activity that they think is amazing, they will tell everyone they possibly can.

Why? Partly because they love the ability to influence. Being the first to introduce a fun, new trend means that person is a trendsetter, it means they are cool. It feeds to Gen Y's desire to be important and be noticed by others. It is also partly because it is simply so easy to spread the word that it takes minimal effort on the individual's part to spread that message. **When it only takes a few clicks or a quick mass text message, the question becomes, "Why *not* tell everyone about this?"**

While Gen Y is quick to jump on these trends and enjoy them feverishly and aggressively, they are just as quick if not quicker to drop them. A large number of members of Gen Y grew up with Baby Boomer parents who did well for themselves and could supply their kids with ample toys and activities. Combine this well-being with a backdrop of increasing consumerism and incessant commercials for the next greatest toy, and the result is a generation who is used to getting plenty of new toys and new, fun experiences all the time. While this group has matured from the age of playing with building blocks, dolls, and action figures, their new toys are the latest gadgets and the coolest new shoes. The excitement and interest in those new gadgets and toys fades quickly, however, as expectations for a new gadget, a new toy, a new shiny object, arise. As the boredom mounts with the old news, the search intensifies for the newest trend. And this generation surely knows how to find that trend.

It is a dynamic and constantly changing lifestyle in which an item is bought one minute and thrown out the next, and a trend is popular one month and is made fun of just one month later. Critics may call it fickle or needy, but this generation has high expectations and correspondingly higher criteria for satisfaction. Out with the old, in with the new. For Gen Y, change is constant.

Why should it be any different? This generation is young. They are still thirsty for new experiences and opportunities for personal growth and enrichment. While this generation is maturing and increasingly entering the workplace, there is still a young, ambitious mentality that is prevalent here, a mentality that there is still so much out there to see and experience, so much to uncover and share. Generation Y has grown up with tremendous outside expectations and predetermined definitions of success. They've always felt pressure and work fast and furious to satisfy and please parents, bosses, and themselves. They grew up flourishing with lives lived at a decidedly frantic pace, and even as they age, they do not want to that pace to slow down. Work is not enough, but rather work, play, travel, and party...and *maybe* a few hours of sleep. Growing up does not mean Gen Y's lives cannot still be exciting and full of new adventures and experiences.

As Gen Y continues to get older then, their story further develops into a truly unique composition of a variety of shorter stories. Comfortable childhoods and an upbringing of consumerism have led to an energetic adoption of the latest trend and an eternal search for the next big thing. At the same time, outside expectations had led Gen Y to want to please others and find success. This generation's members want it all, and their restlessness and the frenetic pace at which they live and flourish will continue to lead them in fast-paced and busy lives.

LOOKING AHEAD

Moving forward, then, it becomes increasingly harder to zero in and target this generation. Pinpointing their interests and thinking in their mindset becomes a tougher and tougher challenge, as Gen Y is constantly on the move. Trends and movements must be preempted, predicted, and expected. Keeping up with Gen Y's pace is essential, or they will leave everyone who's too slow in the dust without the faintest look back.

SELF-CREATED

Generation Y may have their hands full multitasking a variety of short stories and living life at a blindingly fast pace, but this generation is making sure it writes and owns its own story. While this may be the most coddled and cared after generation to date, it is also confident and ambitious. **Generation Y is taking its story into its own hands to show the world that while this cohort may have lived comfortable lives and while they may have been swarmed with attention while young, they are growing up and saying confidently, "I am my own person. This is *my* voice." The result is a story more personalized than ever.**

One way in which Generation Y members express themselves as individuals beyond presumptions and age stereotypes is by differentiating themselves from their parents. Without a doubt, this generation's parents have had a tremendous effect on their lives. Baby Boomer parents became helicopter parents, and never before has a generation been paid so much attention or been treated so carefully. Parents and guardians largely protected this group's feelings. Just look at the childhood trophy shelves of Gen Y and it's clear that from schools to little leagues, everyone made each and every Gen Yer feel like a winner. The degree to which Gen Y's' parents care about and involve themselves into Gen Y lives is intense, and leads to multiple results. Gen Y relies on their parents and turns to them often for support, but at the same time, this group flaunts its differences from its parents and lives confidently its own way.

One can argue that to an extent, any generation follows this pattern of having close relationships with parents while maintaining a certain eagerness to separate themselves and come into their own. But Gen Y's confidence means they are finding their own identities and yearning for independence at earlier and earlier ages. Technology has played a role here, where Gen Y kids received cell phones at younger and younger ages and the autonomy that comes with those phones. Kids used computers at younger ages as well, and instant messaging and online gaming sites geared towards children enable Gen Y kids to communicate with each other and socialize at younger ages. Socializing becomes something kids can take charge of on their own instead of through play dates arranged by parents, and so a sense of social independence is instilled in this generation at a younger age. They took control and forged their own relationships early on, finding communities and acceptance. They have carried that empowered mentality into adulthood by continuing to take ownership of their story.

A TROPHY GENERATION

Another reason Gen Y members express independence early on and form their own unique identities at younger ages is because one of the byproducts of Gen Y's parents paying these Gen Yers so much attention as kids is confidence. They may be naïve, but they do think they're right. Sure, the coddling means this generation will run to their parents in a tight spot. But they've also grown up with tremendous support and tons of compliments, which means this group feels good about itself. All those childhood trophies on the shelf mean confidence and attitude for this group. People also taught Gen Y from a young age that they should value and foster self-expression, and it is encouraged and even enforced through mandatory participation in school. When a student's grade depends on speaking out and voicing one's opinion, it's no wonder this generation is confident and tells stories.

Combining unflinching parental support with the reinforcement of self-expression in schools and communities reveals one certain thing: this generation has personality, and they've been raised with the tools to tell their own story in their own voice.

Gen Y has values, too. They have had plenty of morals and ideals instilled in them, and because they are so close to their parents, they more often than not accepted their parents' values as their own without much thought or fight. The attention paid to them throughout their lives means they will not be easily willing to compromise or abandon those values or morals. They are stubborn and expect a lot, and with so many remote outlets of personal expression – the internet, cell phone, etc. – Gen Y has found a way to express these personal values behind the safety of a computer screen. Gen Y publicizes what for previous generations may have been deeply personal values and opinions. This generation talks about anything and everything in the constant search for identity through consensus, validation, and community.

THE PROGRAMMED GEN Y

All of the attention, assurances, and gratification that adults showered upon Gen Y while they grew up lead to a unique and somewhat paradoxical result: Gen Yers strongly seek stability, direction, and a chance to please, while at the same time desire freedom and channels of self-expression and creativity.

Gen Y grew up with lives planned meticulously by their parents: trumpet practice on Monday, Karate on Tuesday, Soccer on Wednesday, and religion study on Thursday. Gen Y parents took unprecedented control over so many aspects of Gen Y life that as this group has aged, they have continued to search for and depend on that stability and that guiding direction every step of the way. Their lives have been so programmed that they have a strong desire to please those parents, educators, friends, and others who give them attention and praise. They want to hear they're doing a great job from day one; they expect it. This generation hates ambiguity because they never dealt with it as kids. Everything was always made clear, always laid out, always guided. After all, this generation loves instant gratification. Gen Y has come to expect this all the time, even in adulthood. This means they expect constant feedback at school and at work, and demand instant results over long waits. Gen Y's mindset is immediate and short-term, and they will sacrifice the long-term for clarity and assurance now.

"I define myself as an empowered young woman who aspires to achieve greatness in her lifetime. It is a bit over the top. But it inspires me to ever

All this helicopter parenting and lavish praise have led this generation to be conservative in terms of wanting stability and direction; they want rules, and they embrace conventionalism.

This is not a generation of revolutionaries, but rather one that wants security, security of a safe, nice, successful life. But despite their dependence on direction and rules, they do not depend on others to tell their story for them. In fact, it is very much the opposite. The fact that parents have protected these Gen Yers and have fought their fights for them means Gen Yers have inflated egos. They do not seek direction, constant feedback, and stability because they doubt themselves; they seek it because they feel *entitled* to it. They feel entitled to having the constant support of others in their efforts to achieve and write their *own* story. They expect direction and stability because they expect support, and with that support, they can find their

"I don't know how to clearly define myself. I could use adjectives and descriptions of my personal history, current status, and future plans, but I don't know if that fully catches the idea of who I am."

own, express themselves freely and become heroes of their own story.

IT'S ALL ABOUT IDENTITY

And make no mistake, Gen Y are the heroes of their own story. This group is in constant search for identity. It's an awkward and uncomfortable process that all youth go through, but Gen Yers are still always looking for communities and groups that make them feel comfortable and right. Overall, Gen Y isn't dropping out of school to go to the ends of the earth to search for the meaning of life. What they are doing is what they've been told young people are "supposed" to do: travel and see the world, try new things, and assorted other youthful clichés. Whether these experiences are strengthening their sense of identity or not remains to be seen. The point is, they're out there right now, trying to figure it all out.

When it comes to identity, Gen Yers want to resist and defy labels, but at the same time they search for and relish in commonalities with others to find those common and accepted definitions of identity. "I'm liberal. I'm a hipster. I'm a rock star. I'm a basketball fan. I'm a chocoholic." It's a delicate and sometimes uncomfortable balance between standing out and fitting in, between pushing boundaries without abandoning others. Gen Y wants to stand out and impress others, but this generation also wants to fit in enough so that they're part of a community. This group wants to be remembered, something that can't be accomplished without a real identity and a wide network of friends. For Gen Y, conformity is taboo; there is *nothing* worse than someone else wearing the same dress to a party, and there is nothing better than having a unique outfit that gets compliments from that valued community of friends. Some Gen Yers view individuality as being different, while others view it as being their true selves. Either way, Gen Y views conforming to others as pathetic and weak, and this generation will fight conformity to look and feel cool, creative, and "real."

It's a delicate balance between standing out without trying too hard, being unique without being fake, and it gets back to the idea of Gen Y's value of authenticity. Trying too hard to be "different" becomes its own sad form of conformity. This generation values having a true, honest identity and having a community who appreciates that identity. This group wants to be remembered, something that can't be accomplished without a real identity and a wide network of friends. So while this generation is not on the front lines of protests, wearing their hearts on their sleeves to show who they are and what they stand for, they instead are finding identity through acceptance and admiration from others and through sharing beliefs and tastes. They like pleasant communication and consensus and find validation of who they are in the networks they are a part of. **It's all part of the search to find a comfortable identity.**

"I rarely use [the internet] to alter my identity, but rather to express it more openly." "I don't think one can change his or her identity, but once can succeed in disguising it."

"I don't think one can change his or her identity, but once can succeed in disguising it."

When Gen Y finds a comfortable space and way to interact with their chosen networks, they express themselves openly, confidently, and frequently. This generation believes that self-expression is not just something good, but something great – something *powerful*.

The power comes from the fact that for Gen Y, it is not enough to have a strong identity. Gen Y wants to make sure it creates, manages, and grows its identity on its own terms. They want to tell their own story, their own way. Gen Y has grown up hearing others constantly talk about Gen Y. Who they are, who they aren't, how they should be raised, how they should be managed... all this outside talk has led Gen Y to want to prove themselves on their own terms. Forget what everyone else is saying, this generation wants to write its own rules.

Luckily, for Gen Y, expressing one's own identity has never been easier. With convenient technologies, expressing oneself and making a name for oneself becomes as easy as creating one's own YouTube video or starting an influential blog. **A more interesting take on technology's effect on identity could be that Gen Y flocks to technology as a tool of expression in part because they can manipulate that expression.** They control how they appear online, whether it is on social networking sites or in videos. They can manipulate, alter, and change their identities in order to tinker with the formula and find what they like best, and so the search for identity becomes more dynamic and more quickly altered and progressed. The computer screen and the cell phone cover become shields behind which Gen Y can hide. They can communicate and share while still protecting themselves. This generation values transparency, but social technology allows these Gen Y users to reveal what they want, when they want, in a completely controlled way. This control is why Gen

Yers share beliefs and values that may have been too personal for older generations to share with hundreds of friends; they have total control and the remote nature of technology protects them. It is this empowerment and flexibility that technology provides that Gen Y relishes, the ability to control one's identity completely and to tinker and change it at will with a few simple mouse clicks. All of this of course comes with consequences and dangers. It becomes easy for Gen Yers to avoid *really* taking a stand, instead just going with the flow and adapting those online identities to avoid healthy conflict and achieve consensus. However, the opportunities for self-expression and for communication and collaboration are endless, and Gen Y is certainly taking advantage of them.

Gen Y is telling its own story. They are finding their networks and expressing themselves. They are thirsty to come into their own and have other generations treat them as equals. While this attitude may seem cocky or simply a product of youthful arrogance, Gen Y's underlying message in its behaviors and goals is noteworthy. This generation has higher expectations for *everything*, and they are sick of people underestimating them. They are growing up, they are hitting the world hard, and they have a burning desire for bosses and others to take them seriously. Gen Y's lives are so hectic, they are bombarded by so much media and consumerism, that their fervent efforts to establish a strong identity and be noticed is an expression of a desire to be talked to honestly, to be treated maturely, to be looked in the eyes and squared up as equals. It's about establishing a strong foundation. It's about finding those who appreciate them, who have things in common with them, and enjoying those relationships. Gen Y

demands and thinks it deserves this respect and community. This may be a large generation, with plenty of blanket labels, but each member of Gen Y has its own identity, its own personality, its own way of identifying with others, and each one of those members wants to make that personality known. **Empowerment is everything, and this group is certainly empowered to differentiate themselves and stand out for *who they are*.** This generation will continue to use their tools and this empowered attitude to further establish that unique identity to please everyone and fulfill those high expectations established by parents, educators, friends, and most importantly themselves. As this group ages, they will continue to solidify a strong, stable identity as a key part of connecting to others and finding the stable and successful lives they desire.

LOOKING AHEAD

Moving forward then, personalization and intelligent conversations become key to reaching this group and garnering their respect. Give them the ability to express themselves and make something their own, and they'll respond. Speak to them intelligently and honestly and they'll more likely be willing to listen. What is important is acknowledging that each Generation Y member is unique and proud and that identity is everything to this group.

REMOTELY SHARED

As one of the prevalent and recurring themes for Generation Y is the seamless connection between technology and personal life, one of the most defining features of Gen Y's story is the fundamental shift in how they share that story. Generation Y grew up with technology and doesn't know life without it. It is not a foreign concept separate from one's identity or isolated to work as it may be for others. Instead, technology has been so ingrained in the daily activities of members of Gen Y that this generation's very definition of technology has shifted. **Technology is no longer just a facilitator or a timesaver, it is self-expression and it's a defining part of these Gen Yers.**

Take one of their phones and it's taking a part of *who they are*. Forget wallets, Gen Yers show their true personality in their technology and in how that technology has become a part of their *identity*. Technology and personal lives are inseparable. They are fundamentally intertwined, and the value of each is lessened without the other. It makes perfect sense then, that when it comes to telling its story, Gen Y is flocking to new technologies

"When I went abroad last semester I went through a two week period where I wasn't anywhere near the internet. If I had a question I couldn't just look up the question online, I had to ask people instead. [It wasn't] really a bad thing, but then you limit yourself to what they know or their opinions / perceptions of things."

and is using the internet in new and creative ways to share that story faster, with more people, in increasingly interactive and memorable ways.

WEBAHOLICS

The internet is predictably Gen Y's main vehicle for expressing itself and telling its story. Generation Y is online more than any other generation. According to a Forrester Research report in 2008, Gen Y spends 13.9 hours online each week for personal and work purposes, compared to 9.5 hours weekly for all ages of adults, meaning Gen Y is online almost 50% more than all adults are.[35] In terms of sheer quantity of time spent online, then, Generation Y is the most connected group yet. The percentage of Generation Y members who use the internet is higher than any other generation, as well, with 87% of Gen Y using the internet according to Pew Research.[36] In comparison, the range of Baby Boomers who use the internet is from 70-79%. Compared to older generations, then, the extreme majority of Gen Y is connected, and they're connected for longer periods of time.

These numbers only reveal the tip of the iceberg, however, as the ability to connect to and use the internet from phones and other mobile devices has created an entirely new and extremely convenient way for anyone to access the internet from almost anywhere and at any time. Blackberries and iPhones are gaining huge popularity with Gen Y, and they are putting the investment to good use by constantly using the internet through the phone. Indeed, a whopping 46% of iPhone users are Gen Y.[37] Generation Y is certainly not using this connectivity just to check email, either. Whether it is instant messaging friends, looking up answers to questions on the spot, or playing interactive online games while sitting in a car, **the ways in which Gen Y takes advantage of this constant connectivity is extremely varied and ever expanding.** It means they never disconnect from the network they've come to trust, love, and identify as part of their own identity.

The fact that Gen Y leads the pack in terms of internet usage is probably not a surprise to many. Gen Y is the first generation born and raised during the internet age. They've been online their whole lives, so it was not a habit and lifestyle learned and acquired later in life but rather a lifestyle into which this generation was born. While older generations may have originally needed time to build a trust for the internet and may have viewed the internet as a tool for specific tasks, Gen Y grew up with an inherent trust and passion for being online. **For Gen Y, using the internet is as natural as blinking an eye.** It's a comfort zone, a familiar world. This is Gen Y's domain, and they're in it all the time.

"I feel cut off from people when my internet breaks down."

Gen Y also has grown up with all the tools to stay connected all the time. Gen Y were first to grow up with laptops and cell phones and other benefits of the digital age. The fact that Gen Y is online and connected all the time is due to the cell phone that's always in their pocket and the laptop that's always in their hands. The vast majority of Gen Y owns these tools, highlighted by a college survey that showed a whopping 97% of college students own a computer and 94% own a cell phone.[38] **This overwhelming ownership of technology is what gives Gen Y access and the ability to be connected all the time.** For the minority who doesn't own computers or cell phones, and for those rare times when those who do don't have access to them, internet access can be found anywhere from libraries to campuses to internet cafes. However, the vast majority of Gen Y is always connected because they've grown up having portable technology with them at all times that provides them with that connectivity.

Being connected 24/7 influences every facet of Gen Y's life. Constant connection has transformed the classroom for the Gen Y student. And with more and more campuses providing wireless access on campus and in classrooms, students are bringing their laptops to class and chatting with friends, surfing Facebook, taking notes in a word document, and looking up lecture material on Wikipedia, all while the professor is teaching. Students expect wireless access everywhere on campuses, and they take advantage of the constant connection to other students, faculty, and administrators. Students are checking their email ten, twenty, thirty times a day, and expect others to do so and communicate promptly. Remember, this generation is about instant gratification, something the internet provides better than anything else does.

At work, one can fill out spreadsheets while perusing MySpace. The internet not only helps get work done, but it also is a break from work. Tell Gen Y to get some work done without the computer on, and it will stun them. **Just like school, the workplace has become inseparable from the internet.** For Gen Y especially, being online is truly ingrained in doing any work. In one survey, Gen Y workers in legal and white-collar professions report spending 8.5 hours a day on a personal computer at work.[39] These Gen Y respondents report spending

6.9 of those hours logged on to an internet browser. In contrast, Baby Boomers report logging on to internet browsers less than five hours each day. While the internet plays a pivotal role in workplaces for many employees of all ages, for Gen Y especially, being at work means connecting to the internet all the time.

Constant connectivity has transformed Gen Y's social lives as well. By constantly being connected, this generation doesn't have to plan. Just jump in the car, jump on the iPhone, look up movie times, buy tickets online, and search for the nearest sushi restaurant to the theater, all while waiting at a red light. Flexibility and the transfer of information mean better, brighter, dynamic social environments for this generation. One of Gen Y's enduring themes is the desire and determination to matter to others and to affect others, and the internet allows this to happen with easy access to broader networks. When organizing a party and inviting huge networks of friends is as easy as a few clicks of a mouse online, the social possibilities for this generation are certainly convenient. See a celebrity and want to show a hundred friends? Take a picture on a camera phone and email it out to everyone in an instant. The internet provides the ability to have conversations with multiple people at any time in an instant fashion. For Gen Y, that means this group can pursue all of its social short stories with the click of a mouse or the push of a button. It means this group can influence others and share its stories by reaching wider networks more easily than ever before.

"Without the internet, I'd be completely lost. My life would be incomplete."

So whether it is school, work, or social life, constant connection to the internet means Gen Y can utilize its benefits to the best of their formidable ability, *everywhere they go.*

What is perhaps most important, however, is that this generation is not only *used* to the 24/7 connectivity but *embraces* it. To others, being connected all the time could be as much a gift as it is a curse. Just take one look at some users' love/hate relationship with their Blackberries, where checking email at ten o'clock at night might seem like a curse. But Gen Y views the constant connection to the world as an assurance, a reality, and an outlet – not a leash. The internet is so much a comfort zone that just the knowledge of being disconnected, even without a pressing need for being online, is enough to ruffle this generation's feathers. They love the constant connectivity because they don't view it as invasive. It's natural for this group, and they embrace the flexibility.

What does Gen Y do with all that time spent online? The answer is, in a word, *everything.* Gen Y uses the internet for the basics – email, search engines, etc. – but also uses it for researching products, scheduling a dinner, reading the news, making travel reservations and booking flights, researching jobs, and rating anything from products to professors. While older

"With just one click, I can figure out where my USPS package was just scanned, what all of my friends are doing this weekend, and what website is advertising the cheapest flights."

generations are likely to use the internet for many of these same purposes, there are a number of online activities in which Gen Y is much more likely to engage. These include watching TV online, playing online games, watching and downloading videos, sending instant messages, using social networking sites, downloading music, and reading and writing blogs.[40] Furthermore, as Gen Y grows older, the numbers of users who bank online, get health information, and make online purchases will continue to rise.

The shift to watching TV online is noteworthy. A gradual shift has seen younger viewers watching less TV than their parents and older generations in favor of watching shows online. Generation Y leads the pack in the use of official TV program web sites, with 33% visiting these sites.[41] In contrast, only 19% of Baby Boomers use these sites. Gen Y users are also significantly more likely to watch a full episode while on a show's website, as opposed to just browsing or watching clips. Sixty-two percent of Gen Y users watch full episodes, compared to only thirty-two percent of Baby Boomers who visit.

While Gen Y's heavy usage of the internet to watch television shows may be counterintuitive to the natural image of a teenager wasting away on the couch in a daze, the shift to watching TV online is a fitting result of the frenetic, fragmented, and extremely busy lives these Gen Yers lead, combined with their love for TV. **Make no mistake, Gen Y still watches plenty of TV from the couch, but even when it comes to traditional television, inventions like TiVo and DVR serve the same purpose as watching TV online – flexibility.** When Gen Y's lives are as busy as they are, they don't have time to work their schedules around TV shows. Instead, they'll watch TV when they choose, and they choose to watch often. Gen Y may be busy and all over the place, but they still love television. This is, after all, a generation that has always been bombarded with consumerism, and it shows in their love for mainstream television. From the latest dramas to the wittiest comedies, this generation loves it all. Whether it's a brief escape from the frantic pace of life or a chance to hang out with friends and watch a show together, **Gen Y loves TV, and flocks to it online**. This is then one example of a technological trend that makes lives easier and more flexible, giving Gen Y easier access to something they enjoy. As expected, Gen Y embraces the convenience. And with the surging popularity of sites like Hulu.com, where more and more shows are legally available in high quality, this shift from traditional TV to TV online is only set to continue to strengthen.

Gen Y has also become the face of user-generated content, which expresses a number of Gen Y's desires. User-generated content allows Gen Y to express their own identity and take ownership of their own story, and it helps them be influential to others, be noticed, and be remembered by sharing that content. User-generated content is a powerful product of self-expression, personalization, and creativity, and the fact that they share this content so extensively through technology and the internet shows Gen Y's extremely social nature. **This self-created content is Gen Y expressing itself and projecting its voice.** It's how Gen Y is telling its story, and this ever-growing plethora of user-generated content expresses the profoundly personal nature of the technologies Gen Y loves.

Fifty-eight percent of Gen Yers create personal content online in a given week, while seventy-one percent regularly consume this original content.[42] Fifty-six percent of Gen Y respondents are making their own entertainment – editing music, movies, photos, etc. – compared to only twenty-five percent of matures. They're not just doing it at home in their spare time, either. At work, 58% of Gen Y white collar and legal professionals report using music playing programs, compared to only 35% of Baby Boomer white collar and legal professionals.[43] Usage of other similar software shows the same trend, as 51% of Gen Y respondents reported using video playing programs at work compared to only 25% of Baby Boomers. Photo editing programs showed a 49% to 28% advantage for Gen Y as well. Lastly, with moviemaker programs, 20% of Gen Y respondents reported using them at work compared to only 9% of Baby Boomers. While these survey results do not distinguish whether these respondents use these applications for personal or work purposes, it is clear that these **Gen Y workers are significantly more likely, in some cases more than twice as likely, to use these creative applications in the workplace than their Baby Boomer coworkers and bosses.** Gen Y workers use these technologies to take ownership of their story at work. It could be as simple as using a music-playing program to rock out to some tunes while filling out a spreadsheet, or it could be Gen Y workers editing videos and photos for an interactive client presentation. Regardless of the purpose, however, Gen Y is clearly taking its creative aspirations into the workplace with conviction.

When it comes to creating and watching videos, these Gen Yers upload and watch each other's videos constantly, and many hope to be the next big hit on YouTube.

More than one in ten Gen Y members actively upload personal videos to the internet, and half of online content viewing among this generation is done on user-generated websites.[44] These Gen Yers love putting their face and identity out there for the world to see, and the ease at which they can create, upload, and share videos makes this an easy reality. With the popularity of video sharing sites like YouTube, someone who's just another teen one day can upload a video and have three million fans the next. Additionally, technologies have made it easier than ever for people to cheaply record their own videos and edit them with user-friendly programs. With more and more computers coming with built-in webcams, recording, editing, and uploading a video from home has never been easier. Gen Y is familiar with these technologies and uses videos as an easy means to express their creativity, humor, and talent. It's a way to be noticed and hopefully remembered, and it's a way to express oneself and take advantage of the empowerment

technology provides.

Sharing music serves the same purpose. The emergence of the social networking site MySpace as a vehicle for aspiring and established musicians to share their music and grow their fan bases makes sharing one's music and talents extremely easier. Many Gen Yers perceive fame as easily attainable by embracing these technological opportunities to reach more people than ever before, and the ability to download songs from the internet has expanded the ways in which companies and users can sell and share music. Fifty-eight percent of Gen Yers download music, compared to only twenty-two percent of Boomers, showing that Gen Y embraces the ability to download music more than other generations.[45] This fits with Gen Y's preference for short stories and a fast-paced life; downloading music provides instant gratification. Just like with video technology, the technology needed to record and share music is becoming more affordable and commonplace with new computers, and so the ability to share music is easier. Like videos, sharing music is both a social act and self-expression – right up Gen Y's alley.

Blogs are another example of the personal nature of Gen Y's favorite technologies. Gen Yers read and write blogs more than older generations: 43% of Gen Y respondents read blogs, compared to 34% of Gen X and 26% of Baby Boomers In terms of creating, 20% of Gen Yers have created a blog, compared to only 10% of Gen X and 6% of Boomers.[46] Gen Y doesn't just read and write blogs at home, either. At work, 42% of white collar and legal professional Gen Y employees report reading blogs, compared to only 19% of Baby Boomers.[47] While only 28% of Baby Boomer respondents thought it was very or somewhat acceptable to blog about work-related issues, a larger 43% of Gen Yers agree. Perhaps because Gen Y have grown up with blogs and are more comfortable with them, they are giving blogs a larger and more active role in the workplace than their older coworkers. **Clearly, whether at home, work, or elsewhere, Gen Yers are entering and engaging the blogosphere with passion.**

Why does Gen Y gravitate toward blogs? Many Gen Yers flock to blogs because they enjoy the perceived honesty and find it refreshing. Blogs are "real," and Gen Y connects with that honesty in the face of so much advertising and corporate speak that this generation has learned to filter with considerable skepticism. Blogs are honest and unfiltered, and reading them can be a breath of fresh air. From a reading aspect, blogs have become one of the main sources of information, from hints about hot new products to reviews and critiques of anything and everything, from teachers to vacation destinations. There are blogs for every interest and every group out there, so these blog communities have become a means for people to meet others who share the same interests and opinions. Blogs can be tremendously social, something Gen Y loves.

In terms of creating, blogs are just another way to express one's identity and opinions, to take ownership of the story. In addition, they're a great way to gain a following and influence others, whether through fashion tips, life lessons, or aimless wanderings that happen to be fun to read. Blogs give Gen Y the ability to speak their mind and have others hear it and provide feedback. The feeling of importance that comes with that is something Gen Y craves.

Simply put, whether creating, reading, or commenting, blogs provide an open and unfiltered dialogue that Gen Y relishes. **They love honesty and they love what's "real," and blogs provide that.** Anyone can express their voice, and anyone can gain followers. Because of this social and expressive nature of blogs, as well as their perceived honesty relative to other sources of information, these blog sites will only continue to get more popular and common with this generation.

Generation Y uses the internet and new technologies in general to communicate, whether it's with a friend, family, or in the workplace. An interesting residual of Gen Y's widespread movement to technology is the changing comfort levels in young people with regard to communication. In one survey, nearly one-half of employers surveyed said that Gen Y workers communicate more through technology than in person. [48] This suggests that **Gen Y may prefer to communicate remotely if possible, rather than in person, a statement to the true dependency this generation has on technology**. Indeed, according to a workplace survey, 69% of Gen Yers report spending more time communicating with their coworkers through email and phone than face-to-face compared to 59% of Baby Boomers.[49] Additionally, according to one Ernst & Young survey, 84% of Gen Yers use technology to avoid having difficult conversations.[50] A traditional manager or parent might find this concerning, instead favoring face-to-face interaction for dealing with most situations, especially the difficult ones. But for Gen Y, texting a boss to answer a work inquiry might seem perfectly normal.

Some argue that Gen Y's dependence on technology hurts their people skills, but many Gen Yers are simply so comfortable using technology to communicate that if they don't see a need to get up and talk in person, it makes perfect sense to just shoot an email or text message and keep working. Technology enables offices and employees to spread out and still interact frequently and easily, and Gen Y's dependency on technology to communicate reflects this increasingly dispersed nature of getting things done. Gen Yers love the efficiency and speed of communicating remotely and grab the opportunity whenever they can. So, not only do Gen Yers often times reject the notion that remote communication can negatively affect relationships, many times they actually view remote communication as an advantage and a beneficial tool. In fact, 74% of Gen Y professional workers believed new technology and software applications have made building professional relationships much or somewhat easier.[51] In contrast, only 69% of Gen X and 58% of Baby Boomers felt the same way. So while Gen Y can still interact face-to-face, they value highly the ability of technology and new applications to facilitate communication, and use that easy communication to help build relationships.

While often times Gen Yers communicate remotely for convenience and speed, they do also use remote means of communication as a way of handling difficult or touchy situations more tentatively and from a safe distance. Emails and text messages allow the receiver the option of planning a response and taking their time. Because remote communication is less invasive, Gen Yers may tend to use it in a difficult situation instead of the more direct face-to-face interaction.

Whether Gen Y is hiding behind their computer screens or whether they're just lazy and prefer to communicate from their desks in a way that is so familiar to them, one thing is apparent: the vast array of new communication methods that Gen Y love means that they are changing basic communication norms, both at work and well beyond.

The much-talked-about social networking craze is one of these communication methods, an online realm that Gen Y dominates, and one that also facilitates communication. Sites like Facebook and MySpace dominate the lives of this group, and checking these social networking sites has quite literally become a significant daily ritual for many Gen Yers. Indeed, 75% of online adults 18-24 and 65% of online teens age 12-17 use these online social networks, compared to only 35% of the entire online adult population.[52] As of February 2009, 43% of users of Facebook, a social networking site with more than 200 million users, were between the ages of 18-25.[53] Not only is the vast majority of online Gen Yers using these social networking sites, they are using more than one. Fifty-one percent of social network users have two or more online profiles. Some users may have multiple profiles because they are using both professional sites like LinkedIn and social sites like MySpace, while others may be keeping up with friends on multiple comparable sites, using MySpace, Facebook, and Ning all at once. Regardless, all of these social networking users are extremely active in taking advantage of what these sites offer.

These sites are just one more way that Gen Y can feel constantly connected with other people – whether it's friends, families, or colleagues. And because Gen Y desires to stay in constant connection, they are accessing social networks no matter where they are. Gen Yers love to go home, grab the laptop, and catch up on what their friends are up to on Facebook or MySpace. At school, just take one walk through a typical college's library and it becomes immediately apparent just how many students take Facebook "study breaks." And at work, Gen Y are accessing these sites as well: 62% of Gen Y white collar and legal professional workers report accessing social networking sites during a typical workday, compared to only 39% of Gen X and 14% of Baby Boomers.[54] Most Gen Yers access these sites more than once a day at work, as well. Gen Y respondents admitted to accessing social networking sites 3.2 times in a typical workday, compared to only 0.4 times a day for Baby Boomer respondents. While older generations may view interacting with these social networking sites as a clear private activity inappropriate for work, Gen Y seems to disagree, accessing these sites daily and frequently.

Are Gen Yers simply wasting their employers' time by surfing their Facebook friends' profiles or following their favorite celebrity on Twitter while at work? Surely, this is sometimes the case. **Nevertheless, more generally, social networking sites blur the line between professional and personal lives, creating a situation where many Gen Yers believe it's perfectly acceptable to access these social networking sites at work and use them for work-related purposes.**

This attitude is evident in the 66% of Gen Y respondents who believe it is very or somewhat acceptable to befriend a colleague on a social networking site, compared to only 38% of Gen X and 56% of Baby

Boomers. Additionally, 44% of Gen Y respondents believe it is very or somewhat acceptable to befriend a client on a social networking site, compared to only 24% of Gen X and 39% of Baby Boomers. For Gen Yers, social networking sites are both personal and professional, and can facilitate relationships in both realms. While plenty of Gen Yers probably know they shouldn't be looking through party pictures on Facebook at work, these young employees are also figuring out ways to use these social networks for a wide variety of benefits, both at home and at work.

Why does Gen Y insist on being on these sites so often? The openness of these online communities and the ease of communication and ease of meeting other people resound greatly with this generation and their desire to widen networks, be noticed and remembered, and constantly be in social contact. These sites provide another way to ensure that members of Gen Y are never disconnected and thus never forgotten.

Gen Y is so comfortable with communicating on these social networking sites that they may not see the limitations and weaknesses of this method of communication. While critics of social network sites may argue that nothing can replace face-to-face interaction, Generation Y has grown up communicating with technology so frequently and for so many reasons that they are comfortable talking about anything online. Indeed, in some situations, Gen Y may be more comfortable talking remotely than in-person, and social networking sites are a good example of this.

"I communicate with my friends mostly through text messages and Facebook chatting. Occasionally we'll talk on the phone, usually just when we are about to meet up somewhere."

Online communication provides a wall to hide behind, a distance to plan words and ensure one comes off well in a conversation. At the same time, this online communication also provides the ability to reveal information and speak openly when it may otherwise be too embarrassing or difficult to say.

Social networks allow users to create a personal profile, and this gives users the ability to control how they appear and what information they share. The distance created through this remote communication acts as both a way for Gen Yers to control their image as well as a comforting factor that allows Gen Y to share and be open. It may be paradoxical, but it's what makes these sites so popular.

Whatever the motives for using these sites, they have come to represent one of Gen Y's more frequently used tools of self-expression and communication. While some may call it narcissistic, Gen Y responds to the ability to use these sites to keep others up to date constantly on its members' personal lives, feelings, emotions, and opinions. Sites like Twitter and Facebook allow users to update others on their current status at any given moment. To older generations and traditionalists, it may seem like an invasion of privacy, a curious habit. But technology has shaped this generation to be resoundingly open, and not only does Gen Y find this form of online personal expression and communication normal, it finds it as an ideal way to express oneself exactly the way they want to, and share it with whoever they like. This group loves knowing what others are up to, and just about everyone in this generation is guilty of

Facebook "stalking" others. It might not be a traditional way to get to know someone, but it's certainly effective in keeping Gen Yers connected with each other.

The variety of ways in which Gen Yers use Facebook to express themselves and share their opinions with others is astounding. Users share and comment on pictures, videos, and other media, and games and other interactive applications also facilitate communication and expression. Beyond sharing personal information like interests, favorite movies, music, religious beliefs, relationship status, "about me," etc., users have taken advantage of the public platform of Facebook and use the site for activism and certain causes. Facebook groups mobilize people against anything from hunger to genocide. A Facebook group called "Feed a Child with just a Click!" has more than four million users, and there are other groups with thousands and millions of members for just about every cause: genocide in Darfur, animal cruelty, equality, disaster relief, and hundreds of others. Some activist groups raise money, while others simply spread information and raise awareness of issues. The effectiveness and merit of these groups is debatable; not all of them are serious, some are hoaxes, and without a doubt, people join these groups without actually doing anything about a particular cause. Gen Yers tend to think they're making a difference by adding the "Causes" application on Facebook, but not quite as many of these supporters actually do anything beyond that click. Nevertheless, Facebook has still undoubtedly become an effective platform for petitioning and raising awareness, because users can invite wide networks of friends to a particular group, and suddenly a thousand users receive invites to join a cause.

So while a Facebook group might not end world hunger, the ten million users who joined petitions against a new Facebook design were effective enough for founder Mark Zuckerberg to write a response and make changes, and groups have effectively brought back TV shows and radio stations. While the half-million users who are petitioning for McDonald's to deliver their food might not exactly be changing the world, Facebook has become a valuable platform for people to speak out on a multitude of issues, and Gen Y is leading the online charge. The danger of course is that Gen Y stops seeing the need to lead the charge on the front line, instead settling to go with the flow and be a surface supporter on Facebook or other sites like freerice.com. It becomes more about fitting in and following the consensus rather than taking a stand and getting things done. Gen Y is not above this, and often falls into the trap of passively agreeing with beliefs – the Iraq War is bad, global warming is an issue, genocide must stop, equality rules, etc. – without challenging others and having healthy conflict. Why delve deep into issues when I can support equality with an application on Facebook? It's a dangerous trap, an example of how Gen Y's desire to fit in, be liked, and get along leads to passive support instead of active voices and leadership. It's still self-expression, but it's self-expression along a popular, accepted, pre-paved path. **Gen Y then faces the challenge of using social networking tools in collaboration with face-to-face and front-line interactions as opposed to using them as a replacement.** If Gen Y meets this challenge, the benefits of efficiency and collaboration that these sites offer to better accomplish goals and get things done is a powerful tool, one that Gen Y expertly knows how to use.

Ultimately, Facebook and similar sites provide Gen Y endless opportunities to form, find, and participate in any and all sorts of groups. In addition to activist groups, Gen Yers use Facebook and similar sites to find all sorts of common interests,

"Stuff that changes / is updated daily best keeps my interest. Always something new on Facebook!"

covering topics that include favorite sports teams, common genealogy, political views, career goals, favorite TV shows, alumni networks, favorite brands, or favorite drink at Starbucks. Another social network, Ning, specifically gathers people around their passions, creating networks for anyone from Harry Potter fans to wind energy advocates. In Gen Y's constant search for and strengthening of identity, the ability to find and join groups of interest and to express opinions and interact with others who share those opinions is extremely appealing. Finding these communities allows Gen Y to express their identities, something they relish. Furthermore, when everyone's friends, family, and colleagues are on the site, these Gen Y users become so attached that they often can't stop using it, even when they try. These social networks have become a pivotal tool that connects Gen Y to its important wide networks of people. **So whether it's making new friends or keeping up with old friends and laughing about that preschool picture that a friend just uploaded, these sites are convenient, accessible, exciting, expressive, and above all *personal*, a combination Gen Y couldn't love more.**

When Gen Yers spend so much time logged in to social networks, it's safe to say plenty of them are also instant messaging at the same time. Some social networks like Facebook have recently incorporated chatting functions, recognizing that this group heavily uses instant messaging to keep in touch with friends and family. In one survey of college students, an impressive 76% used instant messaging, and 15% of those IM users were logged on 24 hours a day/7 days a week.[55] Clearly, a majority of this group use instant messaging, and plenty of them use it extremely frequently. Instant messaging is not confined to college students of Gen Y; at work, this group is logged on and chatting away as well. Gen Y white collar and legal professionals report using instant messaging programs 3.1 hours a day.[56] So, while not all of this time logged in may be used chatting, it's clear that Gen Y workers are also attracted to this form of communication, whether to talk to friends or to talk to other coworkers about work-related issues and projects.

While traditionalists may not see how this method of communication could compare or compete with face-to-face interactions, this generation has grown up with instant messaging and **is so comfortable using it that it is not uncommon to see two people instant messaging from mere feet away from each other**. Whether it's as a discreet method of communication at work or in class, or as a primary means of chatting with friends late at night at home, young people instant message all the time, and use AOL Instant Messenger, MSN Messenger, Facebook Chat, Google Chat, Yahoo! Messenger, and other services to do it. With students and Gen Y employees constantly at computers or on phones, it's no wonder they've come to instant message so much. It is a means to stay in contact with more people and communicate more casually than in person or by phone (not to mention that instant messaging is free). Instant messaging is just one way that Gen Y stays connected to wide networks of people and expresses its extremely social nature, and those benefits, combined with the casual

"I will usually text message because it's informal and pretty non-invasive – if they don't want to respond, or don't have time, they don't have to talk to me."

nature of the technology, makes instant messaging extremely popular.

Text messaging is a similar technology, one that Gen Y has adopted even more enthusiastically than instant messaging. Indeed, text messaging has pervaded Gen Y lives from the moment they wake to the moment they sleep (with a few new messages awaiting upon waking, of course.) One recent survey shows that 69% of consumers 18-30 years old send anywhere from one to ten text messages daily.[57] When almost every single Gen Yer has a cell phone, that 69% adds up to quite a lot of messages. These Gen Yers view their cell phones as extensions of their own hands. They've become such a presence in their lives that Gen Yers don't go *anywhere* without their cell phones. **As such, Gen Y is texting anywhere and everywhere, anytime and all the time.** Even at work, Gen Yers refuse to separate themselves from their cell phones. But while older generations may view mobile phones and all the latest associated frills as a distraction from work, Gen Y views it as essential and inseparable from doing one's work. While 69% of white collar and legal profession Baby Boomers believe "PDAs and mobile phones contribute to the decline of proper workplace etiquette," less than half of Gen Y respondents agree.[58] It's possible that Gen Y employees are simply in denial that these phones distract them and others because they love being connected and texting their friends. However, more generally, Gen Yers *live* through these multi-function phones and cannot live without them.

Texting is a way for Gen Y to communicate casually and non-invasively, and the convenience of it has allowed it to become a valuable tool not just for communication but coordination. Gen Y often waits to plan until the last minute because anything from meetings to Saturday night get-togethers can be easily coordinated in a few seconds with the help of texting. With a simple text message, Gen Y can easily communicate updates from the car about where to meet, current location, ETA, and other information, with efficient and increased coordination the result. For Gen Y, texting is a fun, casual, convenient, and beneficial way of communicating on the go and at any

> *"My cell-phone is important to me because it's my way to keep in touch with my family and friends. Most colleges don't offer phone-lines in the dormitories so the cell-phone is the primary source for phone calls. I remember when cell-phones were first introduced and only those who had the money could afford the big bulky phones. Now, it is accessible for everyone."*

time, and as such, it has become a huge part of how they communicate daily.

Whether it's e-mail (old-fashioned to this group), social networks, instant messaging, text messaging, or any other form of remote communication, Gen Y loves using technology to reach more people, more conveniently, at any time.

GADGET GUZZLERS

Almost every Gen Yer owns a computer and a phone. When looking at college students, virtually all of them own these tools, as 97% own a computer and 94% own a cell phone.[59] The extent to which all those computers and cell phones keep Gen Y connected to the internet at all times and in all places has helped lead to a love affair with the internet that has now also been chronicled. Generation Y's love affair with technology does not stop at computers, phones, and the internet, however. This group loves all sorts of gadgets, and is willing to try any new technology out there.

This group is comprised of some serious gamers.

Whether it's an Xbox 360, a Playstation 3, a trendy new Wii or games online, Generation Y enjoys playing video games. Eighty-one percent of Gen Yers age 18-29 play video games, and ninety-seven percent of teens play.[60] In contrast, only 53% of all adults play these games. Part of this popularity of video games by Gen Y could be due to a large amount of them being current students, as 76% of students play video games compared to only 49% of non-students.

Not just students play video games, however. These games are entering the workplace as well. Thirty-nine percent of white collar and legal profession Gen Yers use gaming programs during work hours, compared to only 28% of Gen X and 14% of Baby Boomers.[61] Gen Yers love video games so much that they're playing them even when they should be doing work – a mark of youth, certainly, but a significant example of just how far-reaching a role video games can sometimes play in Gen Y lives.

So why do Gen Yers love video games so much? One of the reasons why Gen Y enjoys playing video games so much is that improvements and innovations in this industry have allowed video games to extend beyond their past stigma of being for nerds only.

The ability to connect to the internet through these systems allows players to play each other remotely online, so friends can play each other and communicate through the game, all from the comfort of their respective homes. Players can also meet others online and make connections through a common love of a game. Additionally, the ability to make profiles and online identities and compare stats and performance makes video games a social and competitive outlet. Games also stay interesting for longer because users can download updates, modifications, and add-ons to keep games novel.

Online connectivity has born entirely new types of games that leverage Gen Y's social desires: its desire to be remembered, to influence others, and to stay in contact with wider and wider networks. Virtual worlds (computer-simulated worlds) have taken off in various forms, with Gen Y often leading the charge. Massively multiplayer online games such as World of Warcraft are examples of virtual worlds that connect people from around the globe in a social and gaming setting that's exciting and interactive. In addition, while these fantasy virtual worlds carry a certain stigma (read: they're not cool), newer games reach more Gen Yers with their social appeal. These games span from realistic war games to racing games to management games like The Sims and Second Life, in which users can take control of virtual avatars and live virtual lives, interacting with others in a social setting.

While online games and virtual worlds span a variety of interests, they are all clear examples of the type of intensely social, interactive games and worlds to which Gen Y responds. The more realistic, interactive, and exciting these games become and the more opportunities they give Gen Yers to interact and connect with others, the more they will grow. As more and more companies realize the attraction young people have to virtual worlds and online social settings, more online games and virtual worlds are popping up tailored specifically to young people and kids. Online games have endless opportunities for connection and interaction, and Gen Yers love them.

Other innovations to traditional gaming consoles engage players in new ways. The Nintendo Wii has a motion-sensor remote that allows players to be active and put effort into games in a completely new way. Other games like Guitar Hero and Rock Band allow users to participate physically and be more involved in the game. These games offer novel challenges that Gen Y users embrace with open arms.

In short, recent innovations and online connectivity have allowed video games to become extremely social. Gen Yers flock to this social nature and connectivity, using it as an opportunity to connect with and expand their networks and as a chance to influence others and be remembered. Seeing one's own username at the top of that online scoreboard is a way to be recognized and even revered by others, something that was previously impossible when video games couldn't access the internet. Now users build entire

communities around these games, and Gen Y are flourishing in them and fighting their way to the top, one victory, one hour, one joystick move at a time. Add to this competitive and social opportunity the customization and personalization options available now (users can do anything from customizing backgrounds to creating their own levels and choose outfits for characters) and video games have found a potent, winning combination. As long as these games continue to provide an opportunity to use cool technology in a social setting with personalized options and fresh updates, Gen Y will keep on playing.

Generation Y isn't referred to as the iPod Generation for nothing. This group has always led the charge on portable music devices and mp3 players, ditching CDs once those hip iPods started popping up. Sixty percent of college students own an iPod or some sort of portable mp3 player.[62] Portable music players like iPods have everything Gen Y wants: portability, control over organization, and the instant gratification of putting songs on the device with a few clicks of a mouse. Gen Y wants music whenever and wherever, and devices like iPods enable this easy access. Whereas having constant access to hundreds or thousands of artists would previously mean carrying hundreds or thousands of CDs, iPods and similar players now put all of those options in the palm of one's hand. The convenience and additional options that come with this capability give Gen Y more control with less effort. This generation has short attention spans and is used to constant stimulation. They multitask constantly and demand entertainment. Music on the go in the form of a sleek mp3 player or pink mini iPod gives Gen Y that access to constant entertainment and stimulation.

From video games to iPods to digital cameras to gadgets like the Kindle, which gives users the ability to access and read materials digitally in a portable device, Gen Y can't get enough of the latest gadget, the new cool toy. These technologies make Gen Y stand out, make their lives easier, and give them flexible and often social entertainment, and as long as that continues, **Gen Y will continue to lead the charge on adopting new technologies.**

PORTABLE POWER

So what do all these Gen Y supported technologies have in common? One major theme is portable power. **The increasingly portable nature of the newest technologies allows Gen Y to take their technologies on the go, giving them more flexibility and more control.** As previously stated, almost all college students own their own computers, and for Gen Yers in general, a laptop has become a best friend. The portable nature of laptops means Gen Y can connect to the internet, do work, play games, and do all sorts of computer activities on the go and in a variety of places, not just at work or at home. Laptops mean computers can go where Gen Y wants to go, and this power and flexibility means Gen Yers can no longer settle for a desktop computer. No longer strapped down or confined by a stationary computer's location, Gen Y is empowered and on the go with their laptops, equipped to move at the blinding speed they love.

The latest cell phones follow the same trend and offer the same benefits, in large part because the latest cell phones are becoming more and more like laptops, offering connectivity, email, games, office applications, and more. Indeed, with the increasing popularity of iPhones and Blackberries, Gen Y has an entire computer in their pocket. Phones are a powerful tool that Gen Y can't live without. That little square in the pocket or purse is Gen Y's constant connection to the world.

Aside from computers and phones, Gen Yers' other technologies are also largely portable. iPods mean music on the go. Digital cameras are necessary to make sure Gen Yers can capture any impromptu experience (to immediately upload, post, and share...). As technology only continues to become more portable, social and communication norms are changing. A good example of these changing norms is the increasing use of laptops and PDAs in meetings. While **32% of Gen Yers view the use of a laptop or PDA during in-person meetings as "essential,"** only 11% of Baby Boomers agree.[63] Similarly, 35% of Gen Yers view the use of these technologies as "efficient" in meetings, only half that number (17%) of Baby Boomers thinks alike. While older cohorts may not be as comfortable using these technologies in new settings just because they are portable, Gen Y is leading the way in using these portable devices to facilitate anything and everything in life. With the power and flexibility they provide, these latest technologies will continue to be alongside Gen Y at all times.

CONVENIENCE AND PERSONALIZATION

What other themes link all these technologies and web activities? In two words, *convenience* and *personalization*. Generation Y will flock to any technology that makes their lives more convenient, that makes life easier. The increased functionality of phones is an example of how having internet access on a phone that fits in a pocket makes looking up information, accessing email, listening to music, etc. all the more convenient. Having a laptop makes doing work on a computer portable and easy. Watching TV on those laptops is more flexible and thus more convenient than having to watch it when it airs on TV. Downloading music is more convenient than driving to the record store. The list can go on.

Secondly, Gen Y will connect with any technology that enables self-expression and personalization, the ability to feel an ownership and a personal connection with a technology will create that valuable link that Gen Y craves. User-generated content is an obvious area where Gen Y can personalize everything online. The ease with which anyone with internet access can create and upload videos, music, and other content has led to Gen Y actively and passionately creating their own content. The ability to customize and personalize social networks to fit one's interests perfectly is another example. The increased customization of video games is yet another area where the ability to personalize a product resonates. Even laptops are becoming increasingly customizable, with customers able to pick their own individual computer parts and have unique decorations and coverings. Gen Y responds to customization and the ability to express one's uniqueness and personality, a common thread that connects the technologies that Gen Y loves and adopts into their daily lives.

ENERGETIC SHARERS

The result of the widespread use of these convenient and social technologies is that Generation Y is sharing its story with more people than ever before. Remember, this generation loves to share, to influence others, and to make a lasting impression. Technology helps achieve this. Gen Y's instant message and text lists averaged thirty-seven people, compared to only seventeen for all ages.[64] Additionally, when Gen Y finds a TV show that they enjoy, they tell and average of eighteen people about it, compared to only ten for all ages. Even more telling is that word-of-mouth is the biggest reason why Gen Y visits websites.[65] Because technologies make communication so much easier, Gen Y shares anything and everything with larger networks of people. Listen to an average Gen Y conversation and they'll probably name a few television shows, a few movie previews, and a new gossip story about a celebrity. This group loves to *talk*, and technologies make it easy to talk to more people, more frequently, in more ways. See something funny? Just take a picture of it on a camera phone, send it to a friend, and she'll upload it to Facebook in a minute. Ten minutes later, eight friends will have commented on the photo. Sharing is easy, and sharing makes experiences more memorable.

Gen Y's aggressive attitudes about sharing also create a trickle up effect, where **Gen Y influence their older siblings and Baby Boomer parents in purchase decisions and lifestyle changes, especially when it comes to technology**. Grandma needs an easy-to-use computer? Gen Yer grandson to the rescue. Mom wants to add music to her iPod but doesn't know where to start? She'll ask her Gen Y kid to do it for her. Gen Y's familiarity with technology and its overwhelming willingness to share and enthusiasm while sharing has led to this young group being impressively influential. Trends don't just stay within the generation, and as new technologies become popular with Gen Y, they are spreading to other generations as well.

All this sharing truly exemplifies the seamless connection between technology and personality for this generation. For this group, it's not sharing a digital piece of information or an electronic message; it's not simply sharing how-to knowledge about a computer. It's sharing a part of oneself; it's sharing one's identity.

LOOKING AHEAD

Gen Y will continue to be early adopters of new technologies. Trends spread quickly with this group, and as a generation who has grown up with technology as part of their lives, this group is not hesitant at all to try new creations and trailblazing ventures. Gen Y will certainly have high standards and may dump a mediocre idea quickly, but if they find a new technology they like, they will adopt it, share it, and it will trickle down quickly. As the face of many new technologies, this group is aware of their influence on their parents, siblings, and other acquaintances, and the technologies that Gen Y adopts will only continue to spread and gain popularity.

Looking forward then, companies must understand these trends and realize that when reaching out to this group, personalization is key. Enhance the ability of Gen Yers to express themselves, connect with others, and take control, and they'll jump on board. Make their lives easier and they'll listen. As much as this generation talks to others and expresses their opinion, the stakes are high, and companies can flourish or fail based on how well they understand what Gen Y wants.

LIFESTYLE AND AESTHETICS: THE HAPPY ENDING

When it comes to Ystory's ending, Gen Y's focus on lifestyle and aesthetics is attempting to ensure that it's a pleasing one. Remember, one of Gen Y's enduring characteristics is its desire to make a lasting impression on others and to stand out. This contributes to Gen Y's intensely social nature. Because of this, Gen Y is very conscious of looking good; they want to look impressive and they want to live impressive lives. This means aesthetics must be pleasing and noticeable to others.

Another of Gen Y's enduring characteristics is instant gratification, and Gen Y lifestyle reflects this "now, now later" philosophy. Everything from financial choices to eating habits and shopping preferences reflects a lifestyle focused on immediate gratification and pleasing results.

Gen Y is about image, and Gen Y's lifestyle and day-to-day habits reflect this image. Everything, *everything,* is about standing out and being unique. While it may be self-centered and narcissistic to some, this is how Gen Y has been raised and taught, and this focus influences each lifestyle decision Gen Y makes.

PARENTS

They aren't called helicopter parents for nothing. As Gen Yers' parents' hovering has had a tremendous influence on Gen Yers' egos and how they approach their

"My parents are extremely involved in my life in the sense that we are very close, and so we speak frequently and they know basically everything about my life."

"Although I see my parents quite often, they are not heavily involved in the complexities of my life. I make my own

identity and self-expression, it directly affects Gen Y's lifestyle. Whether they like it or not, Gen Y's parents have played and continue to play a significant role in these Gen Yers' identities and lifestyles. Often times, the role is more significant than they are willing to admit.

The term "helicopter parent" first became popular when Gen Yers were going off to college, and their parents were hovering incessantly over their Gen Y children's lives, always on the fringe, always making sure nothing went wrong and there weren't any problems in their children's lives. Even when Gen Y didn't want their parents there, these hyper-protective parents were there anyway. Gen Yers have always had the feeling that their parents are always behind them looking over their shoulders to make sure everything goes according to their plans and expectations. Most people may cringe at the thought of how one's parents used to nag about everything and make sure everything was on the right track, but one would think that these parents would back off a little as time progressed and kids grew up. Well, this isn't the case for Gen Yers, whose parents continue the hover well into adulthood. There are those who agree that the extra attention is out of love, not from lack of confidence, and that watchful parents help in guiding their Gen Yers effectively. The other side of the spectrum argues that Gen Y's helicopter parents are too involved in their kids' lives, babying them to the point that it hinders their children's development by

"I've learned over the years that my parents are NEVER wrong. Now I never doubt their words of wisdom."

over-sheltering them from many "live and learn" experiences. Regardless of which of these views may be "right," one thing is for sure: their deep involvement has without a doubt helped to shape many aspects of Gen Y's lifestyle and behavior.

Just like everything else in Gen Y's world, the continuous parental hovering has both positive and negative implications. **Gen Yers turn to their parents often for advice on anything and everything, and they depend on and enjoy the support.** On the other hand, that support system comes as a package deal with the added pressure to meet high expectations that parents set from the moment many of these Gen Yers were born. These "helicopter parents" and the ambitious lives they have always had planned out for their Gen Y kids have helped fuel the fire that is Gen Y's drive and competitiveness.

Although Gen Y parents often view the drive and competitiveness that they instill in the children with their hovering in a positive light, the effect on Gen Y's lifestyle is significant. Many Gen Yers feel as if they live in a pressure cooker, believing that they must not only excel within school or work, but in extra activities such as music, sports, or academic teams. It is no longer good enough for a Gen Yer to make straight A's; he or she must also be the captain of the varsity soccer team, the lead in the school play, or a youth group leader at a religious

"[My parents] have instilled a good work ethic in me without pressure me too much to achieve goals that are out of my range. But their views are important to me and I would not want to disappoint them."

institution. For the college-aged Gen Y, a top GPA is no longer enough; the Gen Y must also possess a prestigious internship at a top law firm and be the president of a community-service based organization on campus. Parents often bring out the drive and motivation to accomplish these necessary steps at an early age. The Gen Y parent that plays Baby Einstein for their toddler is often also the parent who puts their teenager through five different SAT courses, rigorous tennis lessons, and signs them up for various youth groups. Helicopter parents want their child to be well rounded and to excel in each area of their life. **Often times, the pressure to excel and the daily grind can drive a Gen Y crazy.**

Gen Yers not only have to deal with this specific pressure from their parents, but they also feel pressure to keep up with the latest social trends and maintain a big, cool group of friends. On top of making great grades, excelling at work, and running various organizations, the Gen Y must also wear the trendiest clothes, own the newest MP3 player, and be a key member of an elite group of friends.

Gen Y parents have hovered and protected their kids, yet have extremely high expectations for them. The result is a generation whose lifestyle is packed full of activities and accomplishments, of both internal and external pressures to succeed.

It's all part of the overarching goal to stand out from the pack, something Gen Y has heard constantly from parents, educators, counselors, celebrities, and pretty much everyone else. All the activities, all the accomplishments, are differentiators. Gen Y's parents want their kids to be unique and to stand out. Just take one look at the trend in children's names over the past hundred years, and this becomes readily apparent. In 1955, 32% of boys received one of the ten most popular names.[66] By 2007, that percentage decreased to less than 10%. The figures for girls tell the same story. In 1955, 22% received one of the ten most popular names; by 2007, less than one in twelve did. Many parents used to name their children so they would fit in with other kids, but for Gen Yers, parents gravitated and continue to gravitate to unique names, hoping their kid will stand above the rest and be a star. Wonder why Gen Yers value stardom and want to be influential and liked by others? The answer is everywhere, even in their names.

AVID SHOPPERS

Generation Y is a generation of avid shoppers. They know what brands and products they want and have no problem exploring various mediums to get them. Gen Y has very high expectations when it comes to the things on which they spend their money. When they find a brand or product they like, they stick with it – unless something cooler comes along. The hardest thing isn't attracting them as a consumer, its keeping their interest and retaining them as a loyal customer. Gen Yers consider themselves very knowledgeable and perceptive shoppers. The internet is the main weapon in their arsenal of information. With the innovations of wireless internet and mobile phone technology, now it is easier than ever to do product research and read reviews. For example, a Gen Yer is inside a retail location wondering if she should buy a product. She decides to pull out her 3G cell phone to read product reviews and compare prices at other retail locations. She checks Amazon.com, reads reviews, sees online prices, and discovers it is cheaper at a competitor's store and even less expensive if she orders it through an online vendor that is offering a rebate coupon. In the past, many people would forego the hassle of driving to different locations to compare prices, which might only save the ten bucks spent on gas driving around. **But Gen Y has the research tools necessary to get a good deal and not settle for less.**

"Anything from shoes to a laptop, I'll shop around and look for the best deal, and I usually shop on the internet because it is easier, typically cheaper, and I can compare many products in a short amount of time. In addition, I can look at customer reviews of the product which makes a big difference in my decisions... Thanks to the internet, consumers are more educated in their purchasing decisions."

Why do Gen Yers love shopping so much? A predictable answer is the consumerist society in which they grew up. It is well chronicled, but Gen Y grew up with more media, more advertising, and more consumerism bombarding them from all angles at all times than any other generation. While there is a countermovement against this consumerism because of the incessant pressures placed upon Gen Y by it, for the most part, Gen Yers embrace the consumerist side of them. Essentially, all

"I love the convenience of being able to go to a store's website and buy what I need and then have it shipped to me."

that marketing worked. Gen Yers may have a love/hate relationship with brands, but the love part wins out more often than not, and Gen Y love buying and talking about brands, too.

The fact that Gen Y talks about brands so much is not altogether surprising. In fact, it fits with their main descriptive characteristics quite nicely. Gen Y is about image and the search for identity: for acceptance, for influence, and for being noticed in the right way, by the right people. **Brands play a huge role in creating and expressing that identity.** Gen Y is also obsessed with building networks of people around similar interests because it strengthens a sense of identity and importance, and brands are one such interest. Additionally, with the ease of communication and the social nature of Gen Y, they have more conversations with more people. Love that new Seth Rogen movie? Update a Facebook status or send a mass text, and hundreds of friends hear about it in an instant. Technology's convenience and reach, combined with Gen Y's social nature and desire to influence and belong, means word-of-mouth is huge with this group. When it comes to shopping, Gen Y is getting out there, talking about brands, and sucking up the trendiest and hottest offerings out there.

"Compared to my parents, I am a much more compulsive shopper. I am also very intrigued by new technologies and new products. So when I see something that I don't have, I act like a very spoiled child and feel like I desperately need whatever it is."

Whether it's the coolest new clothing style, the latest iPod, the funniest new movie or the trendiest new shoes, Gen Y is shopping and consuming – whether online or in store – and they're telling their friends about it every step of the way. Shopping and brands are a huge part of Gen Y's lifestyle, as it helps them find and express their identity, share it and connect with others, and be noticed and influence people in their wide networks. It's materialistic, but it's a visual way of telling their story, and Gen Y is taking full advantage.

So what do Gen Yers buy? What do they shop for and why? When it comes to lifestyle, Generation Y is all about everyday luxury. This generation wants it all, and that means luxury that is available and affordable. Sure, plenty of Gen Yers are suckers for that designer bag or that Rolex watch. But overall, Gen Y wants value; they expect trendy and nice without paying a fortune for it.

As a young generation that cares so much about image, this makes a whole lot of sense. Gen Yers are young and don't have a ton of money, but they gravitate so strongly to name brands because they are highly visible badges of class. They show style, personality, and are a status symbol. As a generation that loves to influence others and feel connected to others, having those signs of luxury helps affirm their social status.

"If I feel like I cannot live without it, or if it will make my life significantly easier, I'll probably get it."

Gen Yers want to be cool, and cool means having a trendy apartment without paying a fortune for it. Pay a ton of money for that cool couch? That's just pretentious. Pay too little for that junky one? That's just lame. But find a reasonable price for a simple, trendy looking three-seater? Now that's cool. For Gen Y, it's about having and consuming nice things, luxurious things, without feeling the guilt of emptying the wallet for them. Gen Y wants to enjoy life, and that means living well without going broke doing it. So while this generation is young and can't afford a million dollar apartment and wardrobe, that's not about to stop Gen Y from wanting and expecting to live well and look good.

Yes, this generation loves the balance between affordability and luxury, and that balance has become this generation's definition of trendy and hip —nice, but not flashy. Cool, but not expensive. This leads Gen Y to look for *simplicity* and *convenience*. In their fast-paced lives, the last thing they need is complications. Add to these reasons the recent green movement that preaches excess as a sin, and simplicity becomes a make-or-break attribute. Simplicity also works well with the fact that Gen Y wants honesty and respect when spoken to by brands and companies. Gen Y perceives simple and clean as honest and responds to that honesty. This generation has been so bombarded with media and advertising its entire life that they can sniff out the tiniest lack of authenticity from a mile away. Affordable luxury, then, comes to mean simple and authentic but also stylish; convenience, but also high integrity. It's an example of Gen Y wanting it all.

"I sometimes get caught up with wanting something new or better but electronics get outdated so quickly I get caught up with buying newer models of things I may have already had. A lot of times I buy them because I think they will make some aspect of my daily routine

This strong trend toward everyday luxury and simplicity is shown in Gen Y's most trusted brands – Apple, Trader Joe's, Jet Blue, In N Out, Whole Foods Market, Target, H&M – notice a trend? All of these brands are one of Gen Y's top ten trusted brands, and they all offer affordable luxury in some form, they all stress simplicity and honesty in their offerings.[67] Customers praise Apple for having simple products with cutting edge, stylish design at competitive prices. Trader Joe's and Whole Foods offer a chance for Gen Yers to pick up that chunk of gourmet cheese or a healthy dinner, paying a few extra bucks to look healthy and trendy. Organic is authentic, and Gen Y responds to that.

A burger joint like In-N-Out Burger may not tap into the authentic, organic side of Gen Y, but their quality, reasonable price, and limited menu offerings show that simplicity, convenience, and product quality create an attractive combination for Gen Yers. Jet Blue also has limited offerings in terms of its services and flights, but its in-air service and

"I think the main reason I buy things is to either make me more comfortable or make my life easier."

high quality entertainment, seats, etc. give Gen Y that luxury it desires. IKEA strikes the same balance to become another Gen Y favorite. IKEA trades off some basic expectations like furniture assembly and delivery, but offers simple, compelling, and often creative design. Affordability and luxury. Simplicity. Again and again.

Even the one car brand in Gen Y's top fifteen trusted brands has these same attributes. Volkswagen's gradual shift upmarket to offer more luxury brands has struck a chord with Gen Y; Volkswagen now has its trademark unique designs and style, with higher quality and luxury, at competitive prices.

Target may be a superstore, but it's perhaps one of the best examples of a company that has won over Gen Y with the perfect balance between quality and price. Target's has simple offerings with enough style to avoid being bland. They promote more upscale, trendy purchases compared to other mass merchandisers, without sacrificing on price. This makes Target a Gen Y favorite. Popular Gen Y clothing brands reflect the same balance. H&M's objective? "Fashion and quality at the best price."[68] Abercrombie & Fitch, another popular Gen Y brand, has the phrase "casual luxury" as its theme.[69] What about Starbucks, the holiest of holies? Perceived as higher quality, with a strong, cool image, at a price Gen Y can afford. Additionally, with a Starbucks on every corner and on-the-go offerings, the convenience factor is obvious.

In each one of Gen Y's favorite shopping choices and brands, affordable luxury is apparent. **Simplicity, luxury, authenticity, and value – the key to Gen Y's shopaholic heart.**

Generation Y's hectic lifestyle has been chronicled well. But somewhere in that hectic schedule, Gen Y finds time to eat and drink, and just like everything else, this generation's eating and drinking habits reflect a number of Gen Y's core characteristics, including its social nature, its image consciousness, and its love for customization and convenience.

Gen Yers' lives are on the go, from extracurricular activities to work, school, and volunteering, Gen Y is constantly moving. They live fast-paced lives with short attention spans, multitasking  constantly and expecting everyone else to keep up. Technology reflects this in its increasingly portable and convenient nature. How Gen Y eats reflects on this fast-paced lifestyle as well.

When Gen Yers live such busy lives, there aren't many times when they can sit down and have a leisurely meal. Instead, Gen Yers are snacking fanatics, eating when it's convenient. **Gen Y throws the conventional 3-meals-a-day plan out the window.** Twenty-seven percent of Gen Yers eat a snack or meal between 10:00 p.m. and 5:00 a.m.; a generation too busy to sleep needs some late night fuel.[70] Additionally, an impressive 63% eat a snack or meal between two and five in the afternoon. Gen Yers eat at unconventional times and grab a bite to eat whenever they can, even if that means lunch at four o'clock in the afternoon and dinner/breakfast at four o'clock in the morning.

This unpredictable and fast-paced nature of Gen Y's eating habits means convenience is everything. According to one survey, convenience was the second most important factor affecting meals purchased by Gen Y, second only to price.[71] Gen Y wants food that's portable and easy to consume, a desire reflected in the rise of single-portion offerings and individually packaged snacks. Gen Y wants snacks it can stick in its pocket, meals it can run out the door with in hand, and goodies it can eat with one hand while the other does work, drives a car, or talks on the phone. Gen Y also wants food that is available at any time of day. Gen Y consumes so much fast food because it's convenient and it's always available. Food for Gen Y needs to be easy. Convenience makes a world of difference.

Besides being on the go, another of Gen Y's main characteristics is its love for customization. Whether it's a new laptop or a new car, Gen Y loves to customize, and food is no different. Gen Y likes being involved in the process, and wants to be able to customize its food choices. This explains the surging popularity of burrito chains like Chipotle Mexican Grill and Moe's Southwest Grill; they're cheap, they're fast, and they offer Gen Y the ability to customize ingredients and styles of their burrito, quesadilla, or nachos. Additionally, 44% of Gen Yers report adding personal touches to meal purchases, such as add-ons, toppings, or anything else, because Gen Y want to customize their food. [72] Remember this generation loves unique, and that extends to food. They want to make it their own, make it interesting, and make it exactly the way they want it.

This craving for what's unique and what's interesting extends beyond customization to affect the types of foods Gen Yers desire. Thirty-nine percent of Gen Yers shop for "unique foods," and fifty-one percent often eat ethnic foods. Gen Y love interesting and unexpected twists in their food, and they love what's interesting and fun. Unique food is just part of making their story more original and more memorable.

This search for unique food includes organic food, "fresh" products, and "fair trade" goods. Generation Y's environmentally friendly stances and green habits extend to food in large part because organic and "natural" foods are different. They're attention-getters, and they're interesting. They also tap into health trends that have influenced Gen Y growing up. Many Gen Yers want to eat healthily and consume goods that are good for the body. Gen Y is picking up trends like portion control and wellness. Fifty-three percent of Gen Yers seek out foods with vitamins and supplements.[73] Vitamin Water is one of Gen Y's most trusted brands, in large part because the brand taps into Gen Y's love for wellness products and these added-value vitamins and supplements.[74] Natural products and products considered "fresh" also tap into health trends, as well as Gen Y's eternal search for authenticity and honesty. "Freshness" is often associated with quality and authenticity, and Gen Y thus flocks to products that are fresh and natural.

In terms of organics and fair trade products, a full one-fourth of Gen Yers say eating organic is important, while another 15% say consuming fair-trade goods is important.[75] Beyond the product themselves, this trend also includes eco-friendly packaging. Generation Y want to feel like they're making a difference, and they want others to see them making that difference. Gen Y wants to feel good about buying products, and these organic, fair-trade, and natural types of products accomplish this feeling. Fair-trade goods, organic foods, and vitamin and mineral supplements are all part of being healthy and being socially conscious, but they are also part of looking cool, standing out, and forming communities around these topics. They often also fit into the affordable luxury category of premium and differentiated products at a reasonable price. Gen Y embraces the idea of healthy meals, but they especially embrace the idea when that healthy meal comes in a chic new container that catches the eye and makes a statement to the world.

Lastly, Gen Y's eating and drinking habits reflect their extremely social nature. Gen Y love their wide networks of friends, and they love eating and drinking with those networks. **Food and beverage has a social nature, and Gen Y really lives it up.** As busy as Gen Yers are, they also enjoy a chance to socialize. Sixty-three percent of Gen Yers say they enjoy eating when socializing, and eating is often a communal event for Gen Y.[76] Gen Y are also social drinkers who enjoy going out and having a few drinks while socializing. Food and beverage is a chance to connect with others and tell stories, and Gen Y takes full advantage of this opportunity.

Food and drink for Gen Y is about convenience, image, health, customization, socializing, and fun. Like everything else in Gen Yers lives, they expect food to make their story unique and compelling, and their food and beverage lifestyle choices reflect this expectation.

HEALTH AND WELLNESS

The trend toward health and wellness goes far beyond eating habits and food choices and includes a number of significant lifestyle choices and the consumption of a variety of health and wellness products. The health and wellness industry as a whole is growing strongly, in spite of the economic downturn. Retail sales for the consumer packaged goods health and wellness industry rose above $102 billion in 2007, a 15% increase from 2006.[77] While the economic downturn showed some slowing in retail sales, as no doubt some people sacrificed some relatively expensive wellness products first, the industry still reached retail sales of over $112 billion in 2008, a 9% growth from 2007.[78] While functional and fortified food and beverages comprised the largest product segment, the fastest growing segments included natural/organic general merchandise, with 32% growth in 2008 and 21% in 2007, organic foods/beverages, with 18% growth in 2008 and 25% in 2007, and natural/organic personal care, with 7% growth in 2008 and 29% in 2007.[79] Additionally, vitamins, minerals, and herbal and dietary supplements saw 7% increases in both 2007 and 2008. The attraction of Gen Y to the functional and fortified segment is understandable, as Gen Y look for offerings that will improve their health and give them more health options. Just take one look at a college gym and count the number of Gatorades and Vitamin Waters, and this becomes readily apparent. Organic foods' appeal was also discussed in the previous section as trendy, image bolstering, and socially conscious. However, the fast growth of general merchandise, personal care items, and supplements shows that people are buying health and wellness products beyond food and beverage. Looking around, young people are leading this charge.

Natural/organic general merchandise can include anything from pet products to "natural" clothing to organic cleaning supplies, and personal care items include the wide range of "natural" cosmetics that are becoming increasingly available. The wide application of "wellness" to anything from clothing to food to makeup shows that pretty much anything can be grouped under some "health" category. Gen Y's attraction to all of these wellness options is clear when the benefits are considered.

In terms of personal care items, it's been said before and it'll be said again: Gen Y cares about its image. These products help people look good, and Gen Y sucks up all of these trendy, natural cosmetic options, whether it's anti-aging creams or organic shampoos. Especially when it comes to skincare, **Gen Yers care about looking good, from antioxidants to sunscreens, from getting rid of those recent bouts of acne to making sure those wrinkles never set in**. And it's not just for women anymore; the cosmetic health and wellness options for men are quickly becoming just as diverse as for women as Gen Y men become more willing to spend on looking youthful. With more options available than ever before, Gen Y men and women are taking full advantage of a wide array of health and wellness beauty products to make sure they stay young and look good.

"Issues that are most important to me . . . revolve around my personal life. This means physical health, relationships, friendships, mental health."

Vitamins and other supplements also help Gen Yers stay young and look their best. Whether it's high doses of protein to build muscle or supplements that supposedly burn fat, products are out there for anything and everything related to health and wellness.

These products also play into Gen Y's affinity for affordably luxury. Many people consider natural cosmetics and other organic personal care and general merchandise products as premium and luxurious items. Who wouldn't want an organic spa in the comfort of one's own home? As more of these products become do-it-yourself spa treatments, Gen Y will continue to gravitate to these products as luxurious, trendy, and beneficial items that will keep their lives and bodies fresh.

"I think that equality and respect are important issues so I do not appreciate ads that are demeaning to women. The way that women are portrayed in the media has a direct effect on viewers. When young girls are exposed to the extremely thin women in commercials and ads there can be negative effects such as a decreased body image which in turn can lead to dangerous outcomes such as eating disorders. It is disheartening that companies today are more concerned with selling their products than the health and wellbeing of women in our society. There are some positive body image commercials such as the Dove ads that portray average-sized women who are proud of their bodies."

Gen Yers' health and wellness encompasses food and beverage choices and personal care items, but another huge aspect of how Gen Y takes care of its health is wellness from an exercise standpoint. Gen Yers certainly inhabit traditional gyms like everyone else, but young people are also leading the charge in practices from holistic yoga to toxin-cleansing exercise programs to outdoor adventures. Even video games are getting in on the wellness trend, with Nintendo Wii's Wii-Fit, which tracks users' fitness level and provides exercises. For Gen Yers who find simple treadmills too boring, "exertainment" is becoming the new way to stay healthy. Gen Y is full of multitaskers with short attention spans, and when it comes to exercising, they want to be entertained while getting in shape. Gen Y loves experiences, and they feel exercising should be a rewarding one.

This emphasis on the pampering and entertainment side of wellness as opposed to the preventive side of wellness is telling of a number of Gen Y's core characteristics.

For Gen Y, wellness isn't about having health insurance and preventing disease. Instead, it's about pampering oneself, living luxuriously with wellness treatments, and having fun in the process, whether that fun is a kickboxing class or a video game workout. Wellness is about looking good and grabbing attention, and it's also about living well today and getting immediate rewards – that spa treatment was well earned, of course. Whether it's cleansing the body of toxins or just buying organic food because it's the trendy thing to do, Gen Yers are leading the charge in the health and wellness category.

THE GEN Y RELATIONSHIP

With all that time, money, and effort Gen Y puts into looking and feeling good, they're certainly not wasting it by sitting at home alone. This generation wants others to see and like how good they look. It may be superficial, but it's the social acceptance that Gen Y craves, and it leads to an entire new culture of relationships.

"Hooking up? I can't complain. It cuts the awkwardness of the traditional first-date."

Gen Y live fast-paced lives. They have short attention spans. They crave wide networks of friends and want excitement and new things. They are young and restless, and they put a ton of effort into their looks. What is the result of this combination of attributes? A "hook up" culture. Generation Y handles intimate relationships no different from how they handle their hobbies or the latest trends. They're fickle, and they're quick to change. Certainly, a traditional streak runs through Gen Y, one that favors dating, courtship, and romance. But while that traditional streak is there, there remains a prevalent theme with this group, especially the younger segment, of short, quick "hook ups" instead of more serious or traditional relationships. It's short, it's fast, it's exciting, it's

"The hook-up culture frightens me at times. Those who actively partake in the trend seem to completely disregard the potential risks that come along with their actions."

"[The hookup culture] is a little strange but I think that's how it has always been. People are just finally talking about it and giving definitions

new, and it's all about looks and social acceptance.

While this culture may be superficial, most Gen Yers probably view it as simply casual. The possible influences include the usual suspects – risqué advertising, pop culture, etc. – but it really does simply fit with the rest of how Gen Y communicates. Technology and all of the remote communication Gen Y partakes in and relishes means communication becomes more casual and often less personal than ever before. The convenience and flexibility of text messages and Facebook is obvious, but the disadvantage of using these remote technologies to communicate is that these less personal and more fragmented communications replace more personal and intimate means of communicating. Gen Y's "hook up" culture reflects this same impersonal, fragmented, and casual means of connecting with others.

> *"One of the most obvious problems with the hook up culture is the ambiguity of the term hook-up."*

> *"It's kind of degrading sometimes. It's generally clear when you got to a party what people are looking for. And even if guys are nice to girls, they generally have a one track mind."*

Another main reason why Gen Y may favor such casual and impersonal "hook ups" is the fact that Gen Yers love and demand instant gratification. Because they lack patience and want to experience joy immediately, a "hook up" may seem more attractive than anything more long-term may seem. After all, this generation is young, and they have a "fun now!" mentality when it comes to relationships. This generation doesn't have the patience for courtship.

So is the institution of marriage doomed? Is the lust of Gen Y smothering the sanctity of love? Plenty of traditionalists out there are loudly proclaiming these fears and decrying the perceived crumbling of the traditional marriage. After all, out-of-marriage births are increasing, as are divorce rates. But not so fast; the real truth is, while Gen Yers may be young and having fun now, and while they certainly are changing relationship norms, they still hold a number of traditional values when it comes to love and marriage, suggesting that Gen Y's "hook-up" culture" is largely a function of their current age and not their long-term goals.

The hook-up trend is the relationship culture of today's young Gen Yer — they're young, and these relationships are carefree. **But for older Gen Yers who are looking for more serious relationships, and for those Gen Yers who are looking ahead, living together without being married is becoming an increasingly popular option.** Fifty-seven percent of Gen Yers between the ages of 20 and 24 think cohabitation is all right, even if those cohabiting have no interest in considering marriage, while only twenty-four percent disagree.[80] Additionally, more than half of the respondents who were already married had cohabited before marriage. While older generations may have viewed cohabiting before marriage as socially unacceptable or rebellious, Gen Yers view this type of relationship as perfectly normal.

But while some older traditionalists have viewed this rise in cohabitation as a replacement for marriage, cohabiting has not weakened Gen Yers' desire to get married. Instead, cohabiting has naturally evolved as an appealing relationship option due to changing lifestyle structures and the consequent delay of marriage. As "young adulthood" has become a longer and more defined period of many people's lifestyles, during which young people are putting off settling down in favor of career advancement, higher education, and travel, the average age of first marriage has steadily increased. In 1960, the average age of marriage was 20 for women and 23 for men; in 2006, it was up to 26 for women and 28 for men.[81] **With this higher average age of marriages, Gen Yers feel less pressure to get married early, and instead are deciding to live together until they reach an age where they desire to get married.**

This *delayed* desire to get married — as opposed to a replaced desire to get married — is evident in the fact that while only 26% of those between the age of 20 and 24 want to be married now, 83% of those unmarried believe it is important or very important to be married someday.[82] Even those who are currently cohabiting want to be married eventually: 84% of those cohabiting believe it is important to be married someday. They are confident they will be, too, as 70% of respondents say they have a certain or good chance of being married in their early 30's.

Clearly, while Gen Yers are "hooking up" and cohabiting today, they have strong desires to marry in the future and settle down eventually. Of those between the ages of 15 and 24, only 19% of men and 11% of women say they wouldn't mind "at all" ending up childless.[83] In addition, when asked what elements were very important for a successful relationship, 89% of 20- to 24-year-olds said "being faithful," 86% said "love," and 77% said "lifelong commitment." [84] In contrast, only 23.5% said money was important. These figures show **that Gen Y share a number of**

traditional beliefs that older generations also valued about relationships. Gen Yers still want to settle down and have a family. The figures also show that while older generations may have stressed economic security and childbearing as important factors in a relationship, Gen Yers stress emotional factors of a relationship. This suggests that Gen Yers may actually be making mature decisions with their relationships, entering relationships when they are emotionally ready, and the numbers back it up: "The odds of divorce among women who married their only cohabiting partner were 28% lower than among women who never cohabited before marriage."[85]

While cohabitation may represent an option for Gen Yers in young adulthood to choose over marriage, many cohabiting couples and the vast majority of all Gen Yers still hope to marry in the future. While many in this generation are engaging in casual relationships now, Gen Yers still hold a number of traditional relationship values, want to have serious relationships eventually, and know how to take a relationship seriously. They are simply putting off marriage and family goals for later in life because they are ambitious and want to have fun and accomplish other goals before settling down.

ABOUT THE BENJAMIN'S

With plenty of single, non-committed Gen Yers running around out there, they're certainly spending their money and living the life. Gen Y isn't exactly the most financially responsible generation.

The US is a country of consumers who constantly spend, pile up debt, and struggle to save. With the U.S.'s disposable personal income (DPI) at

$10.6 billion and personal consumption expenditure (PCE) at $10.06 trillion, Americans are only saving 1.8% of DPI.[86] It's no surprise why the outstanding consumer credit was a staggering $2.564 trillion in January 2009. This is an increase of 0.8% from Q_4 of 2008 at $2.562 trillion.[87] In one month (Q_4 fourth quarter of 2008 through January 2009), the outstanding consumer credit jumped up by $2 billion. The fact that household debt service payments consume 14% of DPI says a lot about how much money Americans spend that they don't actually have and how much interest they incur because of it. Even though the holiday season most likely didn't help curb credit usage, these numbers still raise a compelling issue: with figures like this, has Gen Y been set up to stumble down a path that will eventually set them farther back than the rest of the country?

Gen Y has a reputation as being naïve or blissfully ignorant when it comes to the subject of personal finance and the financial issues adults face in the "real world", whether it's spending habits, debt, or financial stability. According to the National Foundation for Credit Counseling, 47% of Gen Yers are below average in financial literacy, with little understanding of how to save or budget.[88] Additionally, 45% of Gen Yers have no savings. While these figures are certainly alarming, many of Gen Y's characteristics explain this lack of financial literacy and responsibility. Gen Yers' core attributes – wanting immediate rewards, having a short-term mindset, and focusing on the "experience" – help explain their financial attitudes.

Gen Yers have a "spend now, pay later" mindset, and they spend plenty. They seem to give in to their purchasing desires more easily than older segments of the population. This may be a function of youth, but this group has a significant and lasting weak spot for the flashy purchase. It's not that Gen Y doesn't take into consideration the long-term effects of their spending habits, but rather that they consider those effects and still choose to spend immediately. Gen Yers justify their big spending habits and luxury purchases by believing they deserve the splurge. It's all about the reward: buying that new gadget after acing final exams or nailing a big presentation at work. This plays into the notion of immediate rewards. Gen Yers are more inclined to focus their efforts on goals or tasks where they know their dedication and hard work will pay off sooner rather than later. They work hard, study hard, and in turn want to play hard. They have high expectations when it comes to what they feel they have earned and deserve. This generation is bright, highly educated, and ambitious. Sure, they're worried about their future, but they're more worried about today. It's ingrained in their minds since birth that they are the best, will be successful, and have financial security. Whether people see this mindset as confidence or cockiness, it doesn't matter as long as they can continue to excel, strive for those top dollar salaries, and make sure they put their money where their debt is.

Gen Y's financial situation is a serious concern. **Given their attitudes and spending habits, they might as well be called "Generation Y'D I Spend So Much?" (The D? It stands for Debt.)** The median credit card debt of low to middle-income people from age 18 to 34 is $8,200, and people between 25 and 34 file 22.7% of all bankruptcies in the U.S.[89] Their financial situation may not be as optimistic as their attitudes. As a whole, Gen Y is still spending excessively, piling on debt, and struggling to save.

Gen Y's financial issues have stemmed from a combination of economic and cultural influences. The world today is very different from the world for previous generations, and it in turn has spawned a new generation that reflects these differences. Gen Y grew up in a consumerist society where the cost of getting an education is skyrocketing. Throw these factors into a blender alongside Gen Y's sheltered upbringing and minimal exposure to basic financial education and the result is a generation in debt.

Gen Y's financial attitudes and behaviors can be traced to the consumerist society in which its members were raised, a society that favors indulgence and excess over necessity. It's all about money and living the lifestyle of the rich and famous. Gen Y grew up during a period in American culture that views extravagance and flaunting money, as well as the people who do it, in high regard. Today's pop culture obsessively follows celebrities who spend ridiculous amounts of money on purchases that are flashy and unnecessary. Plenty of young girls idolize heiresses like Paris Hilton because of her extravagant lifestyle and often outrageous behavior. Paris Hilton – a role model? Welcome to a world where a girl who spends dad's money and says nothing but "That's Hot" can become a household name. People can debate the extent to which Gen Y perpetuates and fuels this culture of indulgence, extravagance, and ridiculous lifestyle. Maybe Gen Y is the way it is because of the society it grew up in, or maybe Gen Y strengthened and perpetuates that society by choosing to obsess over people like Paris Hilton. Regardless of who's the chicken and who's the egg, the result is clear: modern culture, media, and entertainment expose Gen Y to the life of the rich and famous and consumerism at every turn, and their spending habits and lifestyle choices mirror this exposure.

It's gotten to the point where having a certain credit card can be seen as the ultimate status symbol. Certain credit cards are so exclusive and mysterious that it requires an invitation and a large amount of wealth to be able to get it. For example, flashing an American Express Centurion Card (more commonly known as the Black Card) at a store is a greater status symbol than the nicest car, watch, or home. The black card is made of aluminum instead of plastic, and only celebrities and very wealthy people have them. There are even rap songs about flashing around an AmEx black card. Gen Yers would do anything for a flashy status symbol, even one as small as a tiny piece of aluminum.

The media embraces these ideals through magazines, radio, and TV programming. There are shows completely dedicated to celebrities and their rich and famous lifestyle. Gen Y loves popular shows like MTV's Cribs and VH1's Fabulous Life, which have the sole purpose of displaying how much money celebrities actually spend to live their extravagant lifestyles. Of course, the newest media development is reality TV. Every network has reality TV programming, and these programs have stretched the definition of the word "reality," as shows continue to push the boundaries of what is appropriate to broadcast on TV. America's reality TV obsession comes from the fact that viewers like to watch people act stupid and embarrass themselves on national television.

Since reality TV shows has reigned supreme on TV, Gen Y grew up watching these shows. The directors of reality TV shows hit the jackpot when they started creating programs that play into Gen Y's characteristics. Gen Y is immersed in media displaying celebrities living the lifestyle they wish to live. **Gen Y grew up watching the most popular reality shows where people do *anything* for money and fame.** Some shows have their contestants eat insects or jump off buildings to win the cash prize. Most of the time, the rules of the competition require contestants to lie and double cross each other in order to win. Gen Y has seen reality show contestants become famous and wealthy for doing nothing except being themselves, even if being themselves means compromising conventional morals. It shows that regardless of education, work ethic, or moral standards, anyone can play the game and be rich and famous. **These shows promote the idea that it is normal to spend a ton of money on luxury items, that there are quick roads to wealth and fame, and that education and hard work are not the only ways to be financially stable and successful anymore.** Like it or not, it's the materialistic culture that Gen Y is used to, and it's what they know.

Today's culture has helped to influence Gen Y's financial attitudes, spending habits, and conceptualization of what it means to be successful. More and more people seem to judge success by the price tag of one's lifestyle and the thickness of one's wallet. However, it's not cash that's stuffing Gen Y wallets, but credit card after credit card.

The concept of spending on credit has gone a long way since its humble beginnings in the mid 1900s as charge cards. With charge cards, one had to pay off the full balance of your charge card at the end of the month. In 1959, companies introduced the alternative of having a revolving balance so that it was no longer required to pay off all your debt at the end of the month, which is more along the lines of the credit cards today.[90] Back then, it was harder to receive approval for a credit card from a big national company. People had to earn credit cards by committing to build their credit. Usually they had to start by financing purchases at a store, then move up and get a gas card. After proving themselves and establishing good credit, then finally they would be able to get a credit card from a national company like American Express or Visa. Once they actually got a credit card, there were strict credit limits that took time to increase. The older generations that include Gen Y's parents and grandparents see credit cards as more of a privilege that comes from and requires responsible spending and financial planning. Gen Y's take? Well, it's just a little different. The evolution of the credit card industry has helped influence Gen Y's financial attitudes and behaviors, so much so that they have a remarkably different perception about the concept of spending on credit than their parents and grandparents.

Today, "plastic" has pretty much replaced all other forms of purchasing, making it easy and tempting to spend. In 2006, there were 1.48 million credit cards swiped in the U.S. By 2010, studies project that number to increase to 1.6 million.[91] Credit cards are now available to anyone and everyone. An eighteen-year old with no job and no credit history, who is still dependent on his parents for financial support, can get a letter in the mail saying he is qualified to get a credit card. Long gone are the days when careful planning and responsible spending efforts earned a credit card. Spending on credit has become so ingrained in today's culture that

ask a Gen Yer what his inalienable rights are and he just might say life, liberty, *credit*, and the pursuit of happiness.

Today's credit card culture is normal and expected for Gen Y because they don't know anything else. Gen Y views credit cards as a necessity, and parents exposed them to their Gen Y kids since adolescence, with parent-funded credit cards for "emergencies only." They do not see credit cards as a privilege or convenience, but rather as something required to survive in daily life. Gen Y likes to use credit because of how simple it makes paying for anything. Driving to the ATM to get cash or mailing a check to pay bills is inconvenient. It is so much easier to make the purchase on a credit card. Online bill-paying features take care of bills automatically; Gen Yers do not even have to remember when to pay their bills anymore. Credit cards have become so convenient and so much of a common practice within Gen Y that they may overlook the importance of planning and responsible spending with this financial tool.

If peer pressure, cultural influences, and convenience aren't tempting enough to get Gen Y hooked on

plastic, the credit card companies specifically target them as a major (and gullible) source of business. The industry has advanced to the point that virtually every business, from banks to companies like Starbucks or Target, offers a credit card these days. Every retailer that Gen Y makes a purchase from asks them if they'd like to open up a credit card account. Upon walking up to the cashier, those familiar words come out: "Would you like to open a (Insert Retailer Name Here) card? You can save 20% now and earn great rewards in the future." Credit card companies are the alligator, stalking its prey, patiently waiting just under the water's edge for the opportune moment to pounce on that blissfully ignorant Gen Yer who can't resist a drink of water. They overwhelm their prey with enticing reward programs, low

minimum balances, high credit limits, and of course the status of being "pre-qualified".

The opportune moment for credit card companies to target Gen Y seems to be when they turn eighteen and head off for college. College acts as a buffer that creates a little bit of space from the constant hovering of their parents. All of a sudden, they are experiencing this newfound freedom away from their parents, which makes it easy and tempting to overspend. Student expenses and college life take a toll on the Gen Y student's cash flow, especially in the present economic downturn, so spending on credit becomes an attractive solution. Gen Y may be vulnerable to overspending on credit during this phase of newly discovered freedom that comes with new options and expenses.

The average credit card balance of a current undergraduate student is $3,173, which is a 46% increase from 2004, and the median debt is $1,645.[92]

The amount of credit card debt increases as students move further along in their undergraduate career. The average credit card debt for college seniors is $4,138, with a fifth of these seniors having a credit balance greater than $7,000.[93] While college comes with expenses, Gen Y is not only using credit cards to pay for educational expenses like textbooks or school supplies but also for non-educational expenses. The top three non-educational expenses that Gen Y puts on credit cards are food (83%), clothing (70%), and cosmetics (69%). These figures show Gen Y's image consciousness and willingness to spend to look good. In college and young life, Gen Y is in completely new surroundings where they have to adapt and enter new social scenes, where having trendy clothes and eating out often is part of this process. Gen Y is piling up debt, but for a justifiable cause in their eyes. They want to enjoy life in the present and worry about the long-term after they graduate.

Approximately 15 million Gen Yers are currently enrolled in undergraduate college or graduate school,

and that number is projected to increase to 2.2 million by the year 2017.[94,95] With the youngest members of Gen Y not yet in college, that 2.2 million increase by 2017 covers the rest of Gen Y that have their sights set on campus. A bachelor's degree is standard today as Gen Yers learn to compete for the highest-ranking universities and continue into graduate school. As competition intensifies for colleges, the cost of getting a good education is skyrocketing. In 2009, tuition and fees combined with room and board for public and private universities increased 5 - 6% in their baccalaureate, master's, and doctorate programs.[96] On top of their credit card debt, Gen Y is borrowing massive amounts of money for student loans. It is estimated that 60% of those who received a bachelor's degree took out loans to pay for their education, and that their average student loan debt increased 18% from 2001 to $22,700 in 2007. As more Gen Yers head into college, graduate school, or professional school, this generation's financial situation may continue to worsen as Gen Y falls into considerable debt.

How did Gen Y come to be this way? Gen Yers' helicopter parents played an integral role in their Gen Y kids' financial attitudes and behaviors. Parents and role models always told Gen Yers they were the best and they'll be successful as long as they worked hard, which influenced their "buy now, pay later" attitude, with many Gen Yers not realizing the importance of saving for future success. Many Gen Yers focus on landing that high-salary job today and assuming it'll pay for the future. Gen Y's parents were and oftentimes still are very involved in their children's lives and aim to provide for them as much as they can. This may be a double-edged sword because on one hand, Gen Y's parents gave their children a great childhood and provided (and in some cases continue to provide) everything they need. On the other hand, if they are not careful they risk the chance of spoiling their children and preventing them from experiencing the life lessons needed to make it on their own. Either way, a large portion of **Gen Y is dependent on their parents for financial support through college and sometimes even into their professional careers.** It's the responsibility of Gen Y's parents to make sure they have passed on to their children the essential skills to survive on their own, like how to create a budget and responsibly manage their money. Nevertheless, Gen Yers have the ultimate responsibility to manage their own money, and for the most part, they're not doing their own research and taking enough initiative.

So if Gen Y's parents didn't always teach them about the importance of money and basic personal finance, who did? This topic seems comparable to sex education. If a parent doesn't feel comfortable speaking with their children about sex, they'll let the school system handle it. Although it isn't as much an issue of being comfortable talking about personal finance, many Gen Yers still didn't learn about saving. Many of Gen Yers' parents may have assumed that their kids' schools would teach personal finance. The problem is that there are currently no federal or statewide government standards or guidelines on the topic of teaching personal finance in the U.S.'s education system, a problem magnified by today's economy.

Gen Y didn't learn about personal finance in school because schools didn't teach it. There are few states out there who address this problem, whether through state legislation or through the state board of education. According to Jump$tart Coalition, a group of organizations who aim to improve the financial literacy of kindergarten through college-aged youth, only three states (Utah, Missouri, Tennessee) require at least a one-semester course devoted to personal finance and only seventeen require personal finance instruction integrated into other course subjects.[97] These programs vary in their requirements and how in-depth the educators must dive into the curriculum. Mostly, it is up to the teacher to use their discretion on how much material they teach about personal finance. These types of programs take years to implement, but they're a start to giving Gen Y some basic saving skills.

Current programs seem to be facing many challenges. Even though 64% of college students said they would have liked to receive financial management information in high school, it seems Gen Y's interest to improve their financial literacy comes later when they are already out of high school and in debt.[98] One high school that offered a class on personal finance canceled it due to lack of student enrollment.[99] Another main hurdle that is slowing down the success of these programs is resource allocation issues. Once the programs get permission to proceed, it takes time to get funding, create course agendas, and train educators. Most require pilot programs to see how effective they are. The problem isn't only the lack of programs supporting personal finance education, it also deals with getting Gen Y students to realize its importance and motivate participation.

As proactive as these efforts may seem, it seems to be too little too late for Gen Y. Since the majority of the state legislation or board of education programs were passed between 2003 to present day 2009, they've already missed the fifty million adults aged 18-29 who had a chance to get their high school diploma, a hefty 60% of Gen Y.[100] As students continue their education into college, there is even more freedom of choosing courses to fulfill major/graduation requirements. **If the Gen Y college student has no interest in taking any type of personal finance class, they may have gone through the U.S.'s entire education system from kindergarten to college without being exposed to the basics of personal money management.**

Will Gen Y wake up? The line between living an expensive lifestyle and actually being able to afford it may be getting a bit blurry. It is justifiable to want nice things earned with hard work, but the difference lies in Gen Y's willingness to spend, the way they want to look, and their future expectations of wealth. Gen Y is comprised of storytellers who live mainly in the present. It is a very image conscious generation. Gen Y sees financial success as an accomplishment that they want everyone to know about. By having nice possessions and living a luxurious lifestyle, even though they may not quite be able to afford it, Gen Y is telling a story about themselves and their future expectations.

But there's always hope. Non-profit and government organizations recognize and try to counteract America's and Gen Y's financial literacy issues. Organizations like the U.S. Financial Literacy & Education Commission and The National Endowment for Financial Education (NEFE) provide financial education resources on their websites for individuals and educators. The American Institute of Certified Public Accountants

(AICPA) and The Advertising Council sponsored a national campaign called "Feed the Pig!", whose goal is to encourage younger Americans like Gen Y to take control of their personal finances.

Feedthepig.org bases its services around a "spokespig", Benjamin Bankes, who reminds Gen Y to feed their piggy banks. The site is interactive and plays well into Gen Y's characteristics, with financial tools, quizzes, and resources that help Gen Y analyze their own spending/savings habits and make changes to better their situation. For example, the website categorizes different types of personalities and spending habits into specific profiles. These profiles help Gen Y decide which "inner under-saver" they are. Selection of a profile customizes the site's other features. The site lets visitors pick which option most applies to them and input their own spending habits and expenses. Then it gives them a visual representation of how much they spend on unnecessary expenses per month or year. Gen Y users can go farther and see how much interest they could have made if that amount of money was in a bank or allocated in other investments. The site also opens visitors' eyes to how personal finances play a role in every life changing situation, like going back to school, starting one's own company, or having children. It's personalized and interactive, playing to what Gen Y likes and maybe – just maybe – teaching them to save a little.

As Gen Y gets older and more members reach adulthood, they are slowly but surely becoming financial realists. It's not exactly an epiphany, but it's at least a slow realization. Two reasons may explain this realization. First, it may stem from the years of compiled debt that now seems harder and harder to pay off. Gen Yers are realizing how much their large amounts of debt may hold them back. Student loans and years of overspending have the adult segment of Gen Y cringing when they realize how much debt they have accumulated over the years. **They are increasingly reaching the age now where they must think about major life decisions, like buying a house or getting married.** These topics cause Gen Y to reevaluate their financial situation because they need to make smart long-term financial goals and commitments.

Secondly, the immediate catalyst of Gen Y becoming more financially aware is the economic downturn; the financial crisis has played a major role in sending Gen Y a much-needed wake up call. For the most part, Gen Y's blissful ignorance and financial illiteracy have gone unscathed until recently. The current economic recession is a huge reason for Gen Yers' slow but steady transformation into financial realists.

As the U.S. government hands out billions of dollars to bail out major automotive and financial service companies,  the job market remains bleak. Every company is feeling the effects of the recession and is reducing their costs, which usually means hiring freezes and layoffs. Gen Y is the youngest and least experienced generation in the workforce, so they are especially susceptible to these consequences. Recent college graduates and those who have been working for only a few years are finding it harder and harder to find and keep jobs. Because of this tough landscape, while critics often accuse Gen Yers of having unreasonable expectations and demands in the workplace, there are signs they are starting to make sacrifices to adapt to today's tougher times. Thirty percent of Gen Yers are prepared to take on more projects or help colleagues with their work so they can keep their current positions, and thirty-three percent are willing to work more hours to improve job security.[101] Forty-four percent rank job security as more important than

"I am worried about not getting a job [given the economy] and maybe getting stuck in a job I dislike. It is important for me to enjoy and feel passionate about what I do and I am worried that I might get stuck in a job that pays well but I do not find interesting."

personal job satisfaction. While these figures are not majorities (clearly not all of Gen Y is willing to make huge sacrifices at work) at least some members of this idealistic generation realize that they can't always have it all.

For those still in school, college serves as a shield to an extent. Unfortunately, the cost of an education and the burden of student loans mean the economic crisis hits college students as well. Seventy-five percent are worried about paying for their college education, and thirty-three percent had no tuition money saved.[102] As the concern mounts, Gen Yers are losing a bit of their idealism about the workplace, instead favoring ways to pay back student loans. In a 2008 survey, 50% of college students would be more likely to accept a job that offers higher pay, but less career satisfaction, in order to repay their student loans.

Don't think for a second that a down economy has turned Gen Y into pessimists, however. **The confidence instilled in this generation is showing in their stubborn optimism in the face of layoffs and mounting debt. As recently as a 2009 survey, 50% of college students and recent graduates feel the job outlook is still positive.**[103] Furthermore, a significant 24% believe the job market is stronger than depicted by the national media. Clearly, while Gen Yers are still as concerned about the economy as everyone else is, they're confident in their own skills.

Still, with no job security, a terrible job market, a bad economy, and high student loans, Gen Y may be finally starting to realize that things aren't so easy and won't be anytime soon. These circumstances are forcing them to be smarter about their financial situation, change their spending habits, and plan for their future. Gen Y is a generation used to change and adapting to new situations. Gen Y is starting to become more financially well informed, and is more than capable to get their finances under control. No one is excited about a recession, but it's the kick in the butt Gen Yers may have needed to teach them some valuable financial lessons.

LOOKING AHEAD

Ystory is redefining how a generation writes, records, and tells its tale. Gone are the days of one central hero. Instead, Ystory has many characters. Gen Y likes to wear a number of faces; one day it's the progressive and political face that's saving the environment, the next it's the multicultural citizen going to college and partying, and the next it's the volunteer rebuilding the Gulf Coast. Gen Y is multi-layered, searching for identity, acceptance, and rewarding experiences, and its many characters achieve this.

Many faces mean many storylines, and Ystory is comprised of many short stories, always starting and stopping and overlapping at once. This multitasking generation has short attention spans, and the result is fragmented, fast-paced, short stories geared to keep Gen Y interested and entertained.

These multiple faces and constant short stories are all in the search for identity and ownership of their story. They know how important a strong identity is in creating a memorable story, and they are empowered to tell that story themselves.

Technology makes creating and telling that story themselves possible. For Gen Yers, technology and personal life are fundamentally intertwined. Technology is identity; it is lifestyle; it is everything. From social networking to portable music, Gen Yers are changing the way people use technology in everyday life, and that technology is changing how Gen Y communicates and lives.

Lastly, Ystory is all about aesthetics and having a happy ending. Gen Yers enjoy living well, and they're spending the money to live that enjoyable lifestyle. This group stresses wellness and looking good. This is Gen Y's story, and they're determined that it be a happy, eye-pleasing, enjoyable one.

This is Gen Y, a group hard to pin down but truly unique. Mainstream but progressive. Safe but ambitious. Idealistic but skeptical. Selfish but reliant on others. This generation is a little bit of everything. They're still growing, still figuring it out, still expanding and embellishing that identity. Ystory is by no means finished; as a young generation, much of the story has yet to be written. Nevertheless, regardless of what the coming chapters bring, Gen Y is determinedly making Ystory one to remember.

EXPERIENCE THE JOY

ACHIEVE SUCCESS

With insights, an understanding of Gen Y's characteristics and the accompanying marketing implications, the ultimate question becomes, "What can you achieve with this understanding?" What exactly is at stake, and what is there to gain? With Gen Y's size, spending power, age, image consciousness, and consumerist, brand-focused nature, the stakes are extremely high and the opportunity is downright huge. Companies who ignore it may crash and burn, but those who listen and communicate effectively with this group can flourish with this next great generation of spenders. Those brands that have already taken off with Gen Y are doing so because they fundamentally understand the way Gen Yers think, feel, and act.

Because of Gen Y's size, companies have everything to gain and everything to lose with this generation. At eighty million strong and currently at ages ranging from early teens to late twenties, this generation is in the process of coming of age and becoming the next great consumer. These people are the children of the Baby Boomers, rivaling them in size. As Baby Boomer parents age, their Gen Y children are taking up their role as the dominant consumer with a great fervor and an unflinching willingness to spend. Furthermore, with a spending power generally estimated at anywhere from two to three billion and only increasing, Gen Y's power in the marketplace is immense.

But Gen Y's direct spending power doesn't begin to tell the whole story. **This group's true influence is often estimated to be anywhere from three to five times its direct spending power.** This generation is tech-savvy and has grown up bombarded by advertising. They flourish in a mainstream consumerist society. They have grown up as product and brand experts and significantly influence older generations on their purchases and new product adoptions. From parents and grandparents to coworkers and bosses, people turn to Gen Yers for help and advice on the latest laptop or the best new phone.

This generation is big, with big money and even bigger aspirations. They're entering adulthood with force and they relish the influence they have on the marketplace, an influence that continues to grow. So back to the question. What can companies achieve? The answer is eighty million customers, eager to influence and willing to spend.

80 MILLION BRAND SPOKESPEOPLE

Gen Y doesn't just represent a purchase. This generation loves to share. They love to talk and influence others. They love to be important. Gen Y knows and naturally utilizes the power of word-of-mouth, and so the opportunity with this generation is not just capturing another customer, but rather capturing a brand spokesperson who comes with a diverse and wide network of people to reach.

Gen Y's profile stresses its social and image-conscious nature. From social technologies to the desire to influence and impress others, Gen Y loves to tell its story and share anything and everything with its wide network of family and friends. This means Gen Y is talking. All the time. And when

plenty of those conversations are about brands, both a brand's risk of disaster and opportunity for success are intensified.

Gen Y *really* loves to talk about brands – members of this generation have 145 conversations a week about brands, which is

twice the rate of all adults.[104] Why does Gen Y talk so much about brands? When identity is everything, brands become a way to express one's identity to others. Talking about a favorite brand can be both a way to fit in or stand out, but either way, it is a personal expression and a way to identify oneself. Gen Y is obsessed with pop culture and consumerism, and brands are a huge part of that obsession. Strong brands help Gen Yers identify with others, influence others, and be noticed and remembered by others. These Gen Y brand conversations span all categories – 75% of teens talk about media and entertainment, followed by sports, recreation, and hobbies (68%), technology (67%), telecommunications (65%), and food and dining (62%). Gen Yers define themselves with brands, and from the latest movie to the newest mp3 player, brands and conversations about them penetrate Gen Yers' lifestyles to the deepest level.

When it comes to conversations about advertising, Gen Y is also leading the way. Fifty-seven percent of teens cite marketing and media in their conversations compared to only forty-eight percent of adults. This generation has been bombarded by media their entire lives, and the result is that media becomes a big part of their lives, a topic of conversation, a way to connect with others.

This eagerness to talk about brands and advertising, to express oneself and connect with and influence others through these vehicles, means **that Gen Yers become not just customers of a brand but spokespeople, what we call BRANDchampions™, for it.** Word-of-mouth is a powerful tool, and Gen Yers can spread a brand's message to hundreds of their friends in a Facebook status or a text message. In addition, while some might assume that people only talk about brands they don't like, 58% of teen conversations about brands are positive. Energetic, authentic, and voluntary brand spokespeople; this asset is what companies can achieve.

A CAUTION – OBSESSED WITH BRANDS, BUT FICKLE, TOO

Gen Yers may be great brand spokespeople, but they often don't realize it. Forty-six percent of teens say they are loyal to brands they really like, but over half say brands "are created by marketers just to get more money."[105] A third agree with the statement, "If there were no brands, the world would be better," but a third also agree that "having cool brands makes me feel cool" and that they are "obsessed with brand names." While this seems contradictory, it may be that Gen Yers like brands and enjoy feeling cool but don't want to admit it, because that's *not* cool. When it comes down to it, Gen Y's story is self-created and focuses strongly on the issue of identity, of individualism and uniqueness. But while this generation knows the important role identity plays in telling its story, it does not always know how to express its true, authentic self, and that's where brands come into play. Brands help Gen Y express its "real" self, its true identity, its authentic definition.

Gen Y may be quick to talk down a bad brand, but whether they realize it or not, they talk about and rely on brands all the time.

SO WHAT BRANDS ARE THEY TALKING ABOUT?

If Gen Y is talking so much about brands, exactly which brands are they representing? Who is getting it right and what are they achieving?

APPLE AND THE SEAMLESS DIGITAL LIFESTYLE

No surprise here. In any conversation about Gen Y's favorite brands, it starts with Apple, a company that has successfully ingrained itself in Gen Y lifestyle to an astounding extent. Apple was one of the first companies to understand and target Gen Y's key core characteristics and desires. Apple understood that for Gen Y, simplicity meant authenticity and translated into hipness. The convenience and design meant Apple's products made Gen Y's lives easier, more portable, and thus cooler.

Apple was also one of the first to understand that Gen Y contextualizes technology in a personal manner. **Technology is not a tool, but rather an ingrained, core component of Gen Y's lifestyle.** Apple understood this, as CEO Steve Jobs began speaking of pioneering a "digital lifestyle" as far back as nine years ago. This digital lifestyle perfectly captures Gen Y, and Apple took advantage of this understanding by offering an array of products that allow Gen Y to have a seamless and convenient digital lifestyle. Apple's products responded to Gen Y's desire and expectation for instant gratification; iTunes and instant downloads enabled Gen Y to get music in a few seconds instead of a trip to the store. Apple's products also responded to Gen Y's desire to feel empowered and to personalize. iPods allowed users to take control over their music, customizing their own playlists, and iPhones provided the vast array of applications to design and choose from that allowed users to take complete control over not just music but an entire assortment of online tools. No other company so effectively captured Gen Y's desire to be empowered as unique individuals. Moreover, with the portable and convenient nature of these products, Apple allowed

Gen Yers to use their products on the go to enable that seamless digital lifestyle that Gen Y demands and loves. In addition, with Apple stores, the company sells all of these products in the same place to show off how their entire product line serves all of Gen Y's needs. Gen Yers want advanced features, limitless customization, *and* extreme simplicity, and Apple struck this delicate balance in their most popular products.

Just how favorably has Gen Y responded to this successful balance, to this accurate response to Gen Y's characteristics, desires, and needs? Apple finds itself atop virtually every "favorite brands" list of Gen Y out there. One survey of Gen Y's fifteen most trusted brands finds Apple at the top due to its products' clean and simple design and its user-friendly nature.[106] Another survey of Gen Y's favorite green brands finds Apple in the top fifteen as well, and while Apple is by no means a pioneer in environmental issues, their simple packaging and simple product design imply greenness due to minimal design and little or no excess.[107] Simple is cool, and Gen Y think Apple reigns supreme. So supreme, in fact, that one survey found that Apple's iPod brand is the brand "absolutely essential to teens."[108] When Apple first released the iPhone, one survey reported that for Gen Y, iPhones were even more desired than a new car. Designed to find the ways youth impress their peers, the survey found that a new car recorded only a 20% popularity rate, compared to 26% for iPods and a whopping 70% for iPhones.[109] Clearly, Apple's products have come to hold a crucial role in Gen Y's lifestyle and in being influential and cool.

Apple is certainly experiencing the joy associated with hitting this Gen Y segment right on the head. In 2004, Apple's net sales were $8.2 billion. In 2008, that number was $32.4 billion, an $8 billion increase over 2007.[110]

Apple's products perfectly meet Gen Y's needs and have become an irreplaceable part of their lifestyle and image. Apple is clearly seeing the financial joy associated with the successful understanding of Gen Y. Add to that the fierce customer loyalty that Apple has generated, and it's a winning package.

MICROSOFT'S RESPONSE

In response to Apple's success with Gen Y, Microsoft has recently begun to catch on to the importance of showing that their products can fit seamlessly into Gen Yers' lives. Windows reached a broad agreement with DIRECTV to allow customers to enjoy digital media across devices; digital content can flow between Windows-based PCs, DIRECTV devices, and XBOX 360 video game consoles. Additionally, Windows Live offerings mean to bring together the relationships, information, and interests that are important on computers and portable devices. Microsoft has its own webpage devoted to Microsoft Live and its "digital life," with links to "enable your digital life."[111] In addition, Microsoft recently announced that it would begin to build its own retail stores, similar to Apple's stores. By providing a place for customers to experience all of Microsoft's offerings, the company can display and highlight the seamless connection between their products and their benefit to users'. And after slowed growth from 2004-2006, where revenue increased $8 billion over that span, Microsoft, since shifting towards a "digital life" concept, has seen revenue grow from $44 billion in 2006 to $60 billion in 2008, twice the increase over the same amount of time.[112]

For both Apple and Microsoft then, digital lifestyle, as driven by Gen Y and the way they use technology, is becoming a major theme in how these companies present their products and services to customers.

These companies understand that Gen Y responds to simplicity, innovation, convenience, and seamless connection to lifestyle, and they are experiencing the joy of having happy, money-throwing Gen Y customers at the door.

WHOLE FOODS MARKET AND TRADER JOE'S – GREEN TRENDSETTERS

While Apple and Microsoft battle to own Gen Y's digital lifestyle, plenty of other companies benefit from Gen Y's other core characteristics. Two other companies who are achieving positive results and experiencing joy from Gen Y are Whole Foods Market and Trader Joe's. Both of these companies understand the kind of shopping experience Gen Yers want, as well as the types of environmentally friendly products they seek out and admire.

Whole Foods Market, a food retailer of "natural" and organic products, has consistently been ranked among the most socially responsible businesses. Whole Foods Market aligns itself with a number of Gen Y's characteristics. The chain only sells products that meet its criteria for "natural" products, which means free of artificial preservatives, colors, flavors, sweeteners, and hydrogenated fats.[113] The chain also seeks out, promotes organically grown foods, and "provides food and nutritional products that support health and well-being." Not only does offering "natural" and organic products fit well with Gen Y's environmentally friendly streak and its desire for green and socially responsible companies, it also fits with Gen Y's desire for all things authentic and "real." "Natural" implies authentic and genuine, which resonates with this generation. The perceived honesty of natural products goes a long way in capturing the Gen Y market. These products also fit with Gen Y's lifestyle obsession with looking good and focusing on wellness, as many consumers perceive Whole Foods' products as better for the body. Lastly, because these organic and natural products are differentiated and often more expensive, Gen Yers view them as more luxurious and nicer than alternatives.

Whole Foods' green initiatives and strategies resonate so strongly with Gen Y that in one survey, the chain came out on top of a list of Gen Y's fifteen favorite green brands.[114] What makes Whole Foods stand out from other green grocery stores and healthy options is that Whole Foods was the first chain to *communicate* greenness to this generation. Whole Foods changed the way Gen Yers thought about food, packaging, and what they carry the products in; Whole Foods was one of the first companies to use reusable sacks instead of plastic bags.

So while Whole Foods is not the cheapest option for grocery shopping, Gen Yers pay the extra charge to get what they want. And Whole Foods is seeing the benefits. From 2004 to 2007, the number of stores increased from 163 to 276.[115] The chain has also seen steady sales increases, with $3.9 billion in 2004 and $8.0 billion in 2008. Whole Foods continues to expand and increase its presence with additional and larger stores, and the company continues to see rising sales, much of which is driven by Gen Y. Whole Foods **understands that Gen Y likes all things authentic, "natural," socially responsible and trendy**, has capitalized on this understanding, and achieved positive results.

Trader Joe's is a similar case. While its positioning is slightly different from Whole Foods – Trader Joe's describes itself as "your neighborhood grocery store" – the store sells many organic and environmentally friendly products. Trader Joe's is known for its employees, who wear fantastically tacky Hawaiian shirts, and for its newsletter, which is quirky and quite different from a standard newsletter. The fun and quirky atmosphere differentiates the company and its stores from more traditional and "rigid" supermarkets, and this more enjoyable shopping experience resonates with Gen Yers, who always look for what's new, unique, and interesting. Trader Joe's offers a variety of gourmet and unusual goods, which taps into Gen Y's desire to be different and treat themselves to indulgences. Trader Joe's has a strong identity, and for Gen Yers who constantly search for ways to express their own identity, Trader Joe's becomes a recognizable name and a way to show one's own personality.

For all these reasons and more, Trader Joe's is a rising star with Gen Y. It was the second most trusted brand behind only Apple, and it was Gen Y's second favorite green brand, behind only Whole Foods.[116,117] The chain is praised for telling environmentally friendly stories about their products using packaging and signs. Gen Y likes Trader Joe's for actively engaging customers about green issues. And Trader Joe's is certainly seeing the benefits of having Gen Y on board. While not a new company, Trader Joe's has exploded in expansion in recent years. From 1990 to 2001, the chain quintupled

"I'm drawn to ads that play toward my sense of humor because I love to laugh. These commercials are also rather subtle, which is also nice, because they aren't in-your-face, loud and obnoxious."

its store count but saw profits grow tenfold.[118] While the chain had 210 stores in 2004, it saw 290 stores by 2007, with revenue of $6.5 billion that year.[119] In 2008, those numbers increased to 326 stores and $7.2 billion in revenue.[120] As Trader Joe's continues to become one of the trendiest brands and continues to expand rapidly nationwide, Gen Y will continue to drive their success by responding to their unique personality, differentiated products, and green products.

Both Whole Foods and Trader Joe's set the trend for communicating directly to consumers about green issues, and both have clear initiatives to support those issues. These companies satisfy **Gen Y's desires for green companies, for "natural" products and wellness, and for unique and fun experiences, and Gen Y supports them in return, giving them the joy and positive growth associated with the backing and word-of-mouth of a generation.**

TARGET & H&M – EVERYDAY LUXURY

Any list of Gen Y's favorite or trusted brands is certainly going to have its share of fashion options, and when it comes to living well at the lowest prices, Gen Y flock to stores like Target and H&M to get their coveted everyday luxury.

As discussed in the Avid Shoppers section, Target's success with Gen Y has been due to its differentiation from other superstores like Wal-Mart and Kmart. Target's offerings are still simple and at a low price, but they have enough style to not be bland. Target strives to offer more upscale, trend-forward merchandise at a low cost, the perfect balance between quality and price that Gen Y expects and loves. H&M strikes the same friendly Gen Y chord with their "fashion and quality at the best price" objective. The clothing store perfectly targets hip Gen Yers by offering cheap but chic clothing.

Key to both of these companies' success at hitting the "everyday luxury" balance is their shared strategy of striking deals – often exclusive – with well-known luxury designers. Target's many exclusive deals include designers like Michael Graves and Fiorucci, and the company also partners with well-known brands like Sony and the Food Network for exclusive collections. H&M's collaborators have included trendy designers like Rei Kawakubo and Roberto Cavalli, with the latest guest designer being Matthew Williamson. When these stores can cut these deals with well-known and up-and-coming designer names without having high prices, they can reap the benefits of designer names without designer prices. So for both Target and H&M, getting trendy, big name designers and celebrities generates buzz, drives shoppers to its stores, and sends Gen Y the message that these products are fashionable and high quality, all while offering their products at prices Gen Y can afford.

One look at the growth of Target and H&M shows the growing popularity of these stores, a growth largely driven by Gen Y consumers. Both chains are rapidly opening new stores; Targets and Super-Targets continue to pop up in communities everywhere, especially those more affluent. The U.S. is already H&M's sixth-largest market less than a decade after the company introduced its first U.S. store. There are three times as many

H&M's in the U.S. in 2008 than there were just five years prior.[121] Additionally, both of these stores are in Gen Y's top ten trusted brands.[122] H&M and Target are clearly seeing the joy of tapping the "everyday luxury" market, and Gen Y consumers are flocking in and out of these establishments' doors to drive that joy.

AMERICAN APPAREL – AUTHENTICITY AND HOW TO BE "REAL"

From digital lifestyle masters like Apple to environmentally-friendly trendsetters like Trader Joe's to everyday luxury offerings from Target, companies are finding success by zoning in on Gen Y's core characteristics and preferences. It's no different when it comes to Gen Y's strong gravitation to all things authentic and "real." Smart companies like American Apparel are taking full advantage by speaking honestly to Gen Y and reaping the rewards.

American Apparel has created controversy with sexually provocative advertising, but these ads have been praised for being honest, without any airbrushing or digital enhancement. **Many ads highlight their subjects' blemishes and imperfections, with personal descriptions attached**.[123] According to American Apparel CEO Dov Charney, all in-store ads are completely untouched.[124] This resonates strongly with Gen Y, a generation that has grown up with so much media, marketing, and advertising thrown at them in an assortment of channels that they have developed sharply critical eyes for advertising speak. Gen Yers are so used to computer-enhanced advertisements and other tricks of the trade that they really respond to an honest and untouched advertisement or message. When they see an ad that they perceive as genuine, as raw and authentic, they are more likely to respond.

Furthermore, this generation focuses strongly on identity, and a large part of that identity is finding ways to express one's true, authentic self. This means plenty of Gen Yers frown upon not only people who are "fake" but companies as well. American Apparel's perceived authenticity gives them tremendous credibility and makes Gen Y inclined to relate to American Apparel's authenticity and adopt its products as part of their own authentic self.

"If you can't truthfully advertise your product, you should rethink that product before you allow us to purchase it and then be disappointed by it."

"I don't like to be badgered by the car salesmen type trying to make a commission. I guess I value honesty."

"My least favorite commercials are ones of testimonials of "real people" – they always look like paid actors and I really am not going to listen to them."

This translates into plenty of joy for the company, with American Apparel making Gen Y's list of their top fifteen trusted brands.[125] Additionally, American Apparel has seen both net sales and gross profit increase by five times in just five years. Net sales have grown from just over $100,000 in 2004 to well over $500,000 in 2008, and gross profit has grown from just over $50,000 in 2004 to almost $300,000 in 2008.[126] In just a few years, American Apparel has grown incredibly fast, and shows no signs of slowing down. Their socially responsible practices and honest, racy advertising has gained much attention and word-of-mouth, and Gen Y is spreading the word quickly and effectively. They understand Gen Y and present themselves as "real" and raw. Gen Y can't get enough.

CUSTOMIZATION – PRODUCTS THAT EMPOWER GEN Y

As much as Gen Yers love authenticity, they also like power. They *really* like power. And that's where customization comes into play. Customization gives users power, and **Gen Y expects the ability to customize anything and everything.** Gen Y is empowered. Its story is self-created, and Gen Yers have continued to develop their own unique identities, whether to stand out and be different or just to find the perfect way to express their true self. The ability to customize anything and everything becomes a powerful tool to express that unique identity. Customization is a way for Gen Y to figure out exactly what they do and don't want and to get the perfect fit for who they are. Customizable products then become perfect symbols and representations of one's identity.

One look at the most revolutionary and successful ideas and products in the past decade lends credibility to this incredible demand for customization. iPods and iTunes, eBay, TiVo, Netflix – the list can go on. iPods and iTunes revolutionized the music industry by giving users the power to customize their playlists down to the very last song. Customers could download songs one at a time if they didn't want a whole album and could make their own playlists. Now, iPods themselves can even come customized with different colors and designs.

TiVo customized the television industry by giving power to the consumer, letting them watch what they wanted, when they wanted, all with the click of a remote. This enabled users like busy Gen Yers the ability to watch TV around their busy schedules. This benefit also holds true for Netflix – unlimited choices at the consumers' fingertips, with the power to create and order lists of movies to rent. In each instance, customization was the key advantage that captured consumers. **No group loves and demands the customization more than Gen Yers, and because of this, they are driving more innovations and products to offer the ability to customize, the ability to design a one-of-a-kind product that can "represent me and only me." MyBrand has come to life.**

Gen Y won't settle, either; they demand constant improvements, constant new ways to customize. Expectations have increased with technology. First, it was customizable cell phone covers, then laptops that can come in various colors, and now one can even go online and design their own shoe or build their own laptop piece by piece. Looking forward, then, the most successful companies will be the ones who can offer Gen Y the ability to customize products and services as much as possible. Give Gen Y the power to make something their own, and they'll adopt it and tell plenty of their friends.

Again, it all comes down to power. Gen Yers are confident and want to take matters into their own hands. They're thirsty to prove themselves and thirsty to customize their lives the exact way they want them.

THE SOCIAL MEDIA PAYOFF

Companies have made great progress in adopting and leveraging social media to help them communicate with the increasing number of customers that inhabit these online social media spaces, spaces dominated by Gen Y. But the question many of these companies seem to be stuck on is, "What's the big payoff?" Essentially, they're all asking themselves, how much joy can social media bring?

The answer is that **success with social media can bring tremendous joy to companies.** Because while people often talk about social media success using criteria like customer engagement, participation, and word of mouth, recent data suggests that financial performance correlates with companies' level of engagement in social media.[127] Companies perform better financially when they more deeply and broadly engage customers across social media platforms.

When engagement is measured based on two criteria, breadth of engagement (number of different touch points) and depth of engagement (level of involvement), the companies who have both strong breadth and depth of engagement in social media outperform other companies from a financial standpoint. Companies with both broad and deep engagement experienced 18% revenue growth in the last 12 months. In contrast, companies with deep but not broad engagement had growth of only 5%, and those with low levels of any engagement had negative growth of 6%.[128] These numbers show that even in a recession, companies with strong commitment to social media experience great financial success, greater than those who don't. And while no direct causation has been proved, these figures are still telling of the fact that financially successful companies are those deeply committed to social media. These companies understand that Gen Yers are using social media and others are following quickly, and that those companies and brands who effectively communicate with them in these spaces will find success.

Starbucks is a perfect example of a company who is experiencing the joy from effectively engaging Gen Y in the realm of social media. Plenty of Gen Yers simply cannot start their hectic daily schedules without first stopping at the nearest Starbucks. But while Gen Y is naturally attracted to Starbucks for its lifestyle image, atmosphere, and coffee, they have also become extremely loyal Starbucks fans in no small part due to Starbucks' ability to engage Gen Yers effectively through eleven different social media outlets.

The centerpiece and foundation of Starbucks' social media presence is the company's MyStarbucksIdea.com, where people submit ideas, comment and vote on those ideas, and keep track of the ones the company is adopting. Starbucks has successfully used this site to engage customers and get them involved in the company. In less than six months after rolling out the site, users suggested more than 75,000 ideas.[129] Users love the ability to influence the company and have a strong voice, and Gen Yers particularly love to have a strong voice. This site caters perfectly to Gen Y's desire for empowerment and influence, and Starbucks has used this platform to have valuable interactions with their Gen Y customers.

Starbucks has since branched out to use a variety of other social media platforms to create additional touch points. Starbucks' Facebook page is one of the most popular pages on all of Facebook, with almost four million fans. Using the fan page as another place where customers can chat with each other and with the company, Starbucks has have huge success with Facebook in creating conversations with customers and building excitement for new products and other events. As an example, the announcement of a new Starbucks mini-card on Facebook led to 1,406 comments and 12,382 people "liking this" announcement.

With all of this activity and success with social media, Starbucks is flourishing. The company averaged 23.4% net revenue growth from 2003-2007, and even in a tough economy in 2008, the company's net revenue still grew 10% to $10.4B.[130] Starbucks is experiencing the financial joy that comes with the company's ability to engage customers, building loyalty, excitement, and an ever-expanding customer base through word-of-mouth and multiple touch points. Social media is at the heart of this achievement.

CONCLUSION

Gen Y's size, spending power, influence, and age make it the next great generation on which companies should have their eyes fixed. **The stakes are high, and companies can either crash and burn with this generation or experience sizable**

rewards. It all depends on how well they understand Gen Y and the core characteristics that drive their lifestyle choices, purchase habits, and perceptions of brands. For companies who understand and effectively target this group, they can experience plenty of joy now and for years to come.

From electronics companies like Apple to grocery stores like Whole Foods to clothing retailers like H&M, companies from a variety of industries and backgrounds have experienced tremendous joy with Gen Y. This joy comes from understanding certain characteristics of this generation and reaching them by offering products and services suited to those characteristics, whether it is their need for a seamless and flexible lifestyle, their social and image-conscious nature, their desire to tell stories and influence others, or their demand for instant gratification.

With Gen Y customers spending money, becoming loyal, and talking extensively to friends and family about brands, the benefits of reaching this group are immense. Gen Yers have a sharp eye and high expectations, but understand their Ystory and *help them tell it*, and there will be eighty million happy customers knocking at the door.

In truth,
Stephen Hom
Analyst

EPILOGUE

The challenge of being able to effectively, credibly and authentically market to the Y Generation, is probably going to go down in history as one of the most difficult challenges for marketers of today.

The confluence of growing multi-culturalism, their need for instant gratification and most importantly, the explosive technological advances in communication technology, has created the "perfect storm" for marketers.

Representing nearly $200 billion in spending power, and influencing nearly another three to five times that amount, the need to understand and better address this group is critical to the success of any company or organization today and going forward.

What is truly fascinating, and honestly, slightly disconcerting from a broader social point of view, is that Gen Y has lost (if they ever have had it), the ability to understand and relate to the idea of human communication and contact as we have known it to be in the past. And though they claim to be politically active and motivated, it is by the push of a keystroke in front of a screen, rather than outside on the front lines. As stated, this is not a generation of revolutionaries, but of passive-aggressives.

When it comes to identity, Gen Yers want to resist and defy labels, but look for the commonalities that define them. Their apparent superficiality in how they handle relationships, "hooking up" and breaking up via a few text taps on their cell, is indicative of how difficult it will be for marketers to create "brand loyals." And while some of the observations we have noted in this book suggest that they do love brands, as we see them freely post comments about their favorite brands on Facebook or Twitter, I wonder how long these "love affairs" will last with those brands? My guess is that they will last as long as their relationships do. **What this means for marketers then is that they need to not be fooled by the apparent acceptance of their brands in**

early stages of the new product life cycle, because as with their relationships, this acceptance is fleeting as they will be always be looking for the next best thing.

Traditional marketing ROI models that historically have helped marketers address overall efficiency, I believe will be virtually irrelevant when discussing or evaluating this group. The idea of lifetime value of this target will be cut short and the longer-term revenues and profits that are garnered through addressing this segment will have to be more focused on the short term. Understanding the effectiveness of how we do things and how our investments are relevant on a short-term basis will be our focus now.

There will be no easy answer to how to market to this segment, but one thing is for sure: **developing marketing plans that have the utmost flexibility and ability to morph with their target, but still stay on strategy with the longer term goals of the brand, will be critical and will be what separates those brands that succeed versus those that do not.**

Enjoy,
Alfredo Ortiz
Partner & SVP

ABOUT RTM&J

RTM&J is a **strategic marketing and management consultancy.** Headquartered in Atlanta, GA, the company is comprised of Fortune 500 executive marketers, corporate strategists, and top-tier consultants. RTM&J delivers high-impact, actionable strategies that move businesses forward. It serves clients large and small, and has helped such major corporations as **Arby's, Cancer Treatment Centers of America, Eli Lilly, Equifax, Google, HC Brill, HSN, IBM, Kellogg's, PacifiCare, Papa-Johns, Russell Corporation, S.C. Johnson, Target Stores, The Coca-Cola Company, The Home Depot, Turner Broadcasting, and Tyson Foods** grow and transform.

The firm's practice areas include brand and business strategy, customer experience, growth and innovation, go-to-market strategy, and micro-segment marketing.

RTM&J's **multi-cultural team delivers a competitive advantage** by providing clients superior service built on a diverse set of experiences. In addition, RTM&J donates 10% of its proceeds to the Real Truth & Joy foundation which supports women in need.

Get to what's Real.

Figure out the Truth.

Do the Marketing.

Experience the Joy.

Find out more at www.rtmj.com.

ABOUT STEPHEN HOM

Stephen Hom is an Analyst with RTM&J and an authentic Gen Yer. Currently a senior at Emory University's Goizueta Business School, he is pursuing a Bachelor's of Business Administration. When he's not in school or at RTM&J, where he began as an intern in 2008, you can find Stephen enjoying music, sports, scuba diving, poker and hanging with friends.

REFERENCES

[1] Kirkpatrick, David D. "Voters' Allegiances, Ripe for the Picking." The New York Times 15 Oct. 2006. 1 Feb. 2009 <http://query.nytimes.com/search/sitesearch>.

[2] Teixeira, Ruy. *The Coming End of the Culture Wars*. Rep. Center for American Progress, July 2009. Web. 29 July 2009. <www.americanprogress.org>.

[3] The American Freshman: National Norms for Fall 2008. Issue brief. Jan. 2009. Higher Education Research Institute at UCLA home of the Cooperative Institutional Research Program. Mar. 2009 <http://www.gseis.ucla.edu/heri/PDFs/pubs/briefs/brief-pr012208-08FreshmanNorms.pdf>.

[4] "CBS Poll: Economy Worries Young Voters." CBS News 21 Apr. 2008. CBS News and MTV Poll. Feb. 2009 <http://www.cbsnews.com/stories/2008/04/21/opinion/polls/main4029859.shtml>.

[5] The American Freshman: National Norms for Fall 2008. Issue brief.

[6] "Young Americans Support Immediate Withdrawal of U.S. Troops From Iraq According to Peanut Labs Gen-Y Survey." Reuters 19 Mar. 2008. Marketwire. Mar. 2009 <http://www.reuters.com/article/pressRelease/idUS201928+19-Mar-2008+MW20080319>.

[7] "91 Percent of Gen-Y Intend to Vote in Presidential Election According to Peanut Labs Gen-Y Political Survey." Marketwire 30 Jan. 2008. Mar. 2009 <http://www.marketwire.com/press-release/Peanut-Labs-815639.html>.

[8] "Young Americans Support Immediate Withdrawal of U.S. Troops From Iraq According to Peanut Labs Gen-Y Survey."

[9] "Natural disasters menace E. Asia."

[10] Experience, Inc. "Four Out of Five College Students and Recent Grads Prefer Jobs at Green Companies." Press release. AllBusiness. 4 Aug. 2008.

Business Wire. Feb. 2009 <http://www.allbusiness.com/labor-employment/human-resources-personnel/11475480-1.html>.

[11] Maritz Poll: Environmentally Friendly Retail Marketing - All Hype or Consumer Preference? Rep. 12 Sept. 2007. Maritz. Mar. 2009 <http://www.maritz.com/Maritz-Poll/2007/Maritz-Poll-Environmentally-Friendly-Retail-Marketing-All-Hype-or-Consumer-Preference.aspx>.

[12] Young, Adina, and Casey Labrack. "Abortion, Economics Key Issues For Young Voters." Washingtonpost.com 29 Feb. 2008. Mar. 2009 <http://www.washingtonpost.com/wp-dyn/content/article/2008/02/29/AR2008022902646_pf.html>.

[13] Teixeira, Ruy. *Culture Wars.*

[14] Teixeira, Ruy. *Culture Wars.*

[15] Teixeira, Ruy. *Culture Wars.*

[16] Teixeira, Ruy. *Culture Wars.*

[17] Steinhauser, Paul. "CNN poll: Generations disagree on same-sex marriage." Cnn.com 4 May 2009. May 2009 <http://www.cnn.com/2009/US/05/04/samesex.marriage.poll/index.html?iref=newssearh>.

[18] Steinhauser, Paul. "Same-sex marriage."

[19] Madland, David, and Amanda Logan. The Progressive Generation: How Young Adults Think About the Economy. May 2008. Center for American Progress. Mar. 2009 <http://www.americanprogress.org/issues/2008/05/pdf/progressive_generation.pdf>.

[20] Madland, David, and Amanda Logan. Economy.

[21] Millenial Makeover. "Democrats Should Act Like the Majority They Are." *Daily Kos.* 23 July 2009. Web. 10 Aug. 2009. <http://www.dailykos.com/storyonly/2009/7/24/757144/-Democrats-Should-Act-Like-the-Majority-They-Are>.

[22] Madland, David, and Amanda Logan. Economy.

[23] Madland, David, and Amanda Logan. Economy.

[24] Teixeira, Ruy. *Culture Wars.*

[25] Teixeira, Ruy. *Culture Wars.*

[26] Greenberg, Anna. OMG! How Generation Y is Redefining Faith in the iPod Era. Publication. 1 Apr. 2005. Www.rebooters.net. Mar. 2009 <http://www.greenbergresearch.com/articles/1218/1829_rebootpoll.pdf>.

[27] Teixeira, Ruy. *Culture Wars.*

[28] Teixeira, Ruy. *Culture Wars.*

29 Pryor, John, and Sylvia Hurtado. 2008 CIRP Freshman Survey: Skills for a
    Diverse Workplace - Pluralistic Orientation. Raw data. 2008 CIRP
    Freshman Survey, Seattle. 22 Jan. 2008.

30 CampusCompare. "Gen Y" or "The Millennials" Gets Wake-Up call with
    Economic Crisis. Publication. 30 Oct. 2008. CampusCompare.
    <http://www.campuscompare.com/survey/economic/>.

31 Stone, Andrea. "'Civic generation' rolls up sleeves in record numbers." USA
    Today 29 Apr. 2009. 29 Apr. 2009 <http://www.usatoday.com>.

32 Stone, Andrea. "Civic generation."

33 Stone, Andrea. "Civic generation."

34 LexisNexis. LexisNexis Technology Gap Survey. Publication. 15 Apr. 2009.
    WorldOne Research. Apr. 2009 <http://www.lexisnexis.com/
    media/pdfs/LexisNexis-Technology-Gap-Survey-4-09.pdf>.

35 DiGiovanni, Myriam. "Tinker FCU Web Site Urges Gen Y to 'Buck the Norm'
    and Make a Budget." Credit Union Times 2 Dec. 2008. Mar. 2009
    <www.cutimes.com/search>.

36 Jones, Sydney. Generations Online in 2009. Publication. 28 Jan. 2009. Pew
    Internet & American Life Project. Feb. 2009
    <http://pewresearch.org/pubs/1093/generations-online>.

37 Enns, Andi. "Tips on How to Market to Gen Y." Sparxoo. 27 Mar. 2009. Apr.
    2009 <http://sparxoo.com/2009/03/27/marketing-to-gen-y/comment-
    page-1/>.

38 Hanley, Michael. "The Challenge of Training the PlayStation Generation." E-
    Learning Curve Blog. 15 May 2009. 20 May 2009
    <http://elearningcurve.blogspot.com>.

39 LexisNexis. Technology Gap Survey.

40 Jones, Sydney. Generations Online in 2009.

41 Knowledge Networks. How People Use Study. "Generation "Y" More Likely To
    View Shows On TV Program Web Sites; Also Gives Greater Consideration
    to Episode Sponsors." Press release. Knowledge Networks. 11 Mar.
    2008. Feb. 2009
    <www.knowledgenetworks.com/news/releases/2008/031108_generati
    on-y.html>.

42 The State of the Media Democracy: Are You Ready for the Future of Media?
    Publication. 14 Apr. 2009. <http://www.deloitte.com/
    dtt/article/0,1002,cid=156096,00.html>.

43 LexisNexis. Technology Gap Survey.

44 The State of the Media Democracy: Are You Ready for the Future of Media?

45 Jones, Sydney. Generations Online in 2009.

46 Jones, Sydney. Generations Online in 2009.

47 LexisNexis. Technology Gap Survey.

[48]CareerBuilder.com. Connecting With Generation Y Workers. Publication. 2008. CareerBuilder.com. Feb. 2009 <www.careerbuilder.com>.

[49] LexisNexis. Technology Gap Survey.

[50]Semuels, Alana. "Hey, boomers: Gen Y thinks you don't get tech." Los Angeles Times 25 July 2008. Mar. 2009 <http://latimesblogs. latimes.com/technology/2008/07/hey-boomers-gen.html>.

[51]LexisNexis. Technology Gap Survey.

[52] Lenhart, Amanda. Adults and Social Network Websites. Publication. 14 Jan. 2009. Pew Internet & American Life Project. Feb. 2009 <http://www.pewinternet.org/Reports/2009/Adults-and-Social-Network-Websites.aspx>.

[53] "US Facebook Users by Age Group (2/1/09)." Chart. MarketingCharts. Feb. 2009. InsideFacebook.com. Apr. 2009. www.marketingcharts.com>.

[54] The State of the Media Democracy: Are You Ready for the Future of Media?

[55] Junco, Reynol, and Jeanna Mastrodicasa. Connecting to the Net.Generation: What Higher Education Professionals Need to Know About Today's Students. 1st ed. NASPA, 2007.

[56] LexisNexis. Technology Gap Survey.

[57]InternetRetailer. "Don't try to reach Gen Y via text messages, says a new survey." InternetRetailer. 10 Aug. 2007. Maritz Research. Apr. 2009 <www.internetretailer.com>.

[58] LexisNexis. Technology Gap Survey.

[59] Hanley, Michael. "The Challenge of Training the PlayStation Generation." E-Learning Curve Blog. 15 May 2009. 20 May 2009 <http://elearningcurve.blogspot.com>.

[60] Lenhart, Amanda, Sydney Jones, and Alexandra R. Macgill. Adults and Video Games. Publication. 7 Dec. 2008. Pew Interent & American Life Project. Apr. 2009 <http://pewinternet.org/~/ media//Files/Reports/2008/PIP_Adult_gaming_memo.pdf.pdf>.

[61] LexisNexis. Technology Gap Survey.

[62] [62] Hanley, Michael. "The Challenge of Training the PlayStation Generation." E-Learning Curve Blog. 15 May 2009. 20 May 2009 <http://elearningcurve.blogspot.com>.

[63] LexisNexis. Technology Gap Survey.

[64] O'Hern, Matt. "Hulu Effect - Youth Want To Watch TV Online, Not Cable." MarketingShift. 19 Dec. 2008. Apr. 2009 <http://www.marketingshift.com/2008/12/hulu-effect-youth-watch-tv-online.cfm>.

[65] The State of the Media Democracy: Are You Ready for the Future of Media?

[66] Jacobs, Gina. Unique Baby Names Not Just a Celebrity Fad. Publication. 20 May 2009. San Diego State University. May 2009 <http://

newscenter.sdsu.edu/sdsu_newscenter/news.aspx?s=71319>.

[67] Gen Y's Totally Trusted Brands. Publication. Apr. 2007. Feb. 2009

[68] H&M. "About H&M." H&M. May 2009 <http://www.hm.com/ us/abouthm__abouthm.nhtml>.

[69] Abercrombie & Fitch. "Abercrombie & Fitch Careers." Abercrombie. May 2009 <http://www.abercrombie.com/anf/careers/brands.html>.

[70] "Crunch Time: Snack-happy Generation-Y'ers are fixated on fun foods that fill the gap between meals." QSR Magazine July 2008. May 2009 <http://www.qsrmagazine.com/articles/menu_development/117/snacks-1.phtml>.

[71] Smith, Jodi L. "A Look Inside Generation Y." Culinology 25 Jan. 2008. May 2009 <http://www.culinologyonline.com/articles/a-look-inside-generation-y.html>.

[72] The Center for Culinary Development. A Taste of CCD's Gen Y Insights. Publication. Oct. 2008. May 2009 <http://ccdsf.com/media/download/CCDGenYResearchHighlights.pdf>.

[73] The Center for Culinary Development. Gen Y Insights.

[74] Gen Y's Totally Trusted Brands.

[75] Smith, Jodi L. "A Look Inside Generation Y." Culinology 25 Jan. 2008. May 2009 <http://www.culinologyonline.com/articles/a-look-inside-generation-y.html>.

[76] The Center for Culinary Development. Gen Y Insights.

[77] Mahoney, Sarah. "Health And Wellness Category Defies Economy." MediaPost. 8 July 2008. May 2009 <www.mediapost.com>.

[78] GMDC. "NMI Reports 2008 Health & Wellness Industry Sales at more than $112 Billion." Www.gmdc.com. 21 May 2009. May 2009 <http://www.gmdc.org/index.asp?w=pages&r=25&pid=59&n=175>.

[79] "Health & Wellness Sales Topped $102 Billion in '07: Study." Progressive Grocer. 7 July 2008. May 2009 <www.progressivegrocer.com>.

[80] Scott, Mindy E., Erin Schelar, Jennifer Manlove, and Carol Cui. Young Adult Attitudes About Relationships and Marriage:. Rep. Child Trends, July 2009. Web. 11 Aug. 2009. <www.childtrends.org/.../Child_Trends-2009_07_08_RB_YoungAdultAttitudes.pdf>.

[81] Scott, Mindy E., Erin Schelar, Jennifer Manlove, and Carol Cui. Young Adult Attitudes.

[82] Scott, Mindy E., Erin Schelar, Jennifer Manlove, and Carol Cui. Young Adult Attitudes.

[83] Wetzstein, Cheryl. "Young Americans plan to be married." The Washington Times. 19 July 2009. Web. 11 Aug. 2009. <http://www.washingtontimes.com/news/2009/jul/19/wetzstein-young-americans-plan-be-married/>.

[84] Scott, Mindy E., Erin Schelar, Jennifer Manlove, and Carol Cui. *Young Adult Attitudes.*

[85] Jayson, Sharon. "Living together no longer 'playing house'" *USA Today*. 28 July 2008. Web. 11 Aug. 2009. <http://www.usatoday.com/news/health/2008-07-28-cohabitation-research_N.htm>.

[86] U.S. Department of Commerce: Bureau of Economic Analysis. "National Income and Product Accounts Table, Comparison of Personal Savings in the NIPAs with Personal Savings in the FFAs." 26 March 2009. <http://bea.gov/national/nipaweb/Nipa-Frb.asp>.

[87] Board of Governors of the Federal Reserve System. "Federal Reserve Statistical Release, G.19, Consumer Credit." 6 March 2009. <http://www.federalreserve.gov/releases/g19/Current/>.

[88] Burton, Christina. "Gen Y Faces Big Financial Learning Curve." *The Wall Street Journal*. 5 Aug. 2009. Web. 11 Aug. 2009. <http://online.wsj.com/article/BT-CO-20090805-709440.html>.

[89] Johnson, Emma. "Why Generation Y is Broke." MSN Money 22 Apr. 2008. 25 Mar. 2009 <www.moneycentral.msn.com>.

[90] Gerson, Emily S., and Ben Woolsey. "The History of Credit Cards." Credit Card News. 18 Dec. 2007. 15 Apr. 2009 <http://www.creditcards.com/credit-card-news/credit-cards-history-1264.php>.

[91] U.S. Census Bureau: 2009 Statistical Abstract, "Credit Cards – Holders, Numbers, Spending, and Debt, 2000 and 2006, and Projections, 2010, Table 1148" 15 Mar. 2009. <www.census.gov/compendia/statab/tables/09s1148.pdf>.

[92] "How Undergraduate Students Use Credit Cards - Sallie Mae's National Study of Usage Rates and Trends 2009." Research. 13 Apr. 2009. Sallie Mae. 21 Apr. 2009 <http://www.salliemae.com/about/news_info/research/credit_card_study/>.

[93] "How Undergraduate Students Use Credit Cards - Sallie Mae's National Study of Usage Rates and Trends 2009."

[94] U.S. Census Bureau, Current Population Survey, "Type of College and Year Enrolled for College Students 15 Years Old and Older, Table 5." 13 Apr. 2009. <www.census.gov/population/socdemo/school/cps2004/tab10-06.xls>.

[95] Hussar, William J., and Tabitha M. Bailey. "Projections of Education Statistics to 2017." IES National Center for Education Statistics. 17 Sept. 2008. U.S. Department of Education: Institute of Education Sciences. 15 Apr. 2009 <http://nces.ed.gov/pubsearch/pubsinfo.asp?pubid=2008078>.

[96] "Trends in College Pricing." Trends in Higher Education Series. The College Board. 2 Apr. 2009 <http://www.collegeboard.com/html/costs/

pricing/index.html>.

[97] State Requirements. Jump$tart Coalition. 13 Apr. 2009.
<http://www.jumpstart.org/state_legislation/index.cfm>.

[98] How Undergraduate Students Use Credit Cards - Sallie Mae's National Study of Usage Rates and Trends 2009."

[99] Fray, Jesse. "Legislation Would Require Finances Classes." LJWorld.com. 6 Mar. 2009. Lawrence Journal-World & 6News. 13 Apr. 2009 <http://www2.ljworld.com/news/2009/mar/06/legislation-would-require-finances-classes/>.

[100] U.S. Census Bureau, 2005-2007 American Community Survey. 15 Mar. 2009. http://www.census.gov/acs/www/.

[101] BusinessWire. "Gen Y Reports Optimistic Attitudes about Work and Value of Education." AllBusiness. 9 Mar. 2009. Experience, Inc. May 2009 <www.allbusiness.com>.

[102] CampusCompare. "Gen Y" or "The Millennials" Gets Wake-Up call with Economic Crisis. Publication. 30 Oct. 2008. CampusCompare.

[103] BusinessWire. "Gen Y Reports Optimistic Attitudes."

[104] Hein, Kenneth. "Teen Talk Is, Like, Totally Branded." Brandweek 6 Aug. 2007. 15 Mar. 2009 <www.brandweek.com>.

[105] Hein, Kenneth. "Research: Teens Schizophrenic About Their Brands." Brandweek 18 June 2007. Viacom's The N Channel. 15 Mar. 2009 <www.brandweek.com>.

[106] Gen Y's Totally Trusted Brands.

[107] Gen Y's Favorite Green Brands. The Green Issue 6. 30 Jan. 2009.

[108] Hein, Kenneth. "Research: Teens Schizophrenic About Their Brands." Brandweek 18 June 2007. 20 Mar. 2009 <www.brandweek.com>.

[109] Mateja, Jim. "Cell Phones Impress Teens More Than Cars." Weblog post. Blogs.cars.com. 6 July 2007. 20 May 2009 <http://blogs.cars.com/kickingtires/2007/07/cells-and-teens.html>.

[110] Apple. 2008 10-K. Rep. 4 Nov. 2008. 7 July 2009 <http://library.corporate-ir.net/library/10/107/107357/items/315133/AAPL_10K_FY08.pdf>.

[111] "Windows Vista and Windows Live. Open up your digital life." Microsoft Corporation. 2008. 08 July 2009 <http://www.microsoft.com/uk/windows/digitallife/default.aspx>.

[112] "MSFT Annual Report 2008." Microsoft Corporation - Selected Financial Data. 2008. 07 July 2009 <http://www.microsoft.com/msft/reports/ar08/10k_fh_fin.html>.

[113] "Quality Standards." Whole Foods Market: Natural and Organic Grocery. 08 July 2009 <http://www.wholefoodsmarket.com/products/quality-standards.php>.

[114] Gen Y's Favorite Green Brands.

[115] Whole Foods Market. 2008 10-K. Rep. 26 Nov. 2008. 7 July 2009 <http://www.wholefoodsmarket.com/company/pdfs/2008_10K.pdf>.

[116] Gen Y's Favorite Green Brands.

[117] Gen Y's Favorite Green Brands.

[118] Armstrong, Larry. "Trader Joe's: The Trendy American Cousin." BusinessWeek 26 Apr. 2004. 6 July 2009 <http://www.businessweek.com/magazine/content/04_17/b3880016.htm>.

[119] The Mediacenter. Scan Report on Health-Food Stores. Rep. Mar. 2008. 6 July 2009 <http://mediacenteronline.com/visitor/DemoSite/ BO_Scans/health_food.pdf>.

[120] "Trader Joe's Market." Supermarket News. 25 June 2009 <http:// supermarketnews.com/profiles/top75/trader_joes_market09/>.

[121] H&M. 2008 Annual Report. Rep. 2008. 6 July 2009 <www.hm.com>.

[122] Gen Y's Totally Trusted Brands.

[123] Wolf, Jaime. "And You Thought Abercrombie & Fitch Was Pushing It?" New York Times 23 Apr. 2006. 6 July 2009 <http:// www.nytimes.com/2006/04/23/magazine/23apparel.html>.

[124] Goodwin, Susan. "An American Dilemma." Oregon Daily Emerald 18 Jan. 2006. American Apparel. 6 July 2009 <http://americanapparel.net/ presscenter/articles/20060118dailyemerald.html>.

[125] Gen Y's Totally Trusted Brands.

[126] American Apparel. 2008 Annual Report. Rep. 16 Mar. 2009. 6 July 2009 <http://investors.americanapparel.net/secfiling.cfm?filingID=1193125-09-55623>.

[127] Engagement Correlates to Financial Performance - Revenue Growth, Gross Margin Growth, Net Margin Growth. The world's most valuable brands. Who's most engaged? July 2009. Raw data.

[128] Engagement Correlates to Financial Performance - Revenue Growth, Gross Margin Growth, Net Margin Growth.

[129] Mguiste. "Groundswell Award." Weblog post. *MyStarbucksIdea: Ideas in Action Blog*. Starbucks, 9 Sept. 2008. Web. 7 Aug. 2009. <http://blogs.starbucks.com/blogs/customer/archive/ 2008/09/09/groundswell-award-application.aspx>.

[130] Starbucks. *Starbucks 2008 Annual Report*. Rep. Nov. 2008. Web. 7 Aug. 2009. <www.investor.starbucks.com>.

4041678

Made in the USA
Charleston, SC
20 November 2009